Other Kaplan Books Relating to Graduate School Admissions

Getting Into Graduate School
Getting Into Business School
Getting Into Law School
Getting Into Medical School
Scholarships
MCAT Comprehensive Review
MCAT Workbook
LSAT
Two Real LSATs Explained
GRE
GMAT
GRE/GMAT Math Workbook

Distance Learning

By Inabeth Miller and Jeremy Schlosberg

Simon & Schuster

Kaplan Books
Published by Kaplan Educational Centers and Simon & Schuster
1230 Avenue of the Americas
New York, NY 10020

For bulk sales to schools, colleges, and universities, contact Renee Nemire, Simon & Schuster Special Markets, 1633 Broadway, 8th Floor, New York, NY 10019.

Kaplan® is a registered trademark of Kaplan Educational Centers. QuickTime™ is a registered trademark of the Apple Computer, Inc. Windows™ is a trademark of Microsoft Corporation.

Project Editor: Richard Christiano
Cover Design: Cheung Tai
Interior Page Design: Michael Syrquin and Jobim Rose
Interior Page Layout and Production: Jobim Rose
Production Editor: Maude Spekes
Managing Editor: Brent Gallenberger
Executive Editor: Del Franz

Special thanks to Kiernan McGuire, Linda Volpano, and Enid Burns

Manufactured in the United States of America
Published simultaneously in Canada

November 1997

10 9 8 7 6 5 4 3 2 1

Library of Congress Cataloguing-in-Publication Data

Miller, Inabeth.
    Kaplan guide to distance learning / by Inabeth Miller.
      p. cm.
    ISBN 0-684-84175-4
    1. University extension--United States. 2. Distance Education--United States. 3. Telecommunication in education--United States.
4. Artificial satellites in higher education—United States.
5. Videoconferencing—United States. 6. Computer-assisted instruction—United States. I. Stanley H. Kaplan Educational Center (New York, N.Y.) II. title.
LC6251.M55   1997
378.1'75'0973--dc21   97-30939
                                             CIP

ISBN: 0-684-84175-4

Table of Contents

About the Authors

Inabeth Miller is Vice President of Academic Affairs at Massachusetts Communications College in Boston, Massachusetts. As a preeminent national expert on matters relating to education and technology, Dr. Miller has served as a member of both the President of the United States Distance Learning Association and President Clinton's Transition Team for Education, and is also a recipient of the Smithsonian–Computer World Award for Outstanding Educator in Technology. Her past accomplishments include a vice presidency at the Lightspan Partnership, which is pioneering educational applications of interactive television, and a four-year tenure as Executive Director of the Massachusetts Corporation for Educational Telecommunications, where she developed the "Massachusetts Learnpike" and established the Commonwealth's leadership role in producing and delivering educational programming through telecommunications. Dr. Miller earned an Ed.D. in Educational Technology and Educational Administration from Boston University, an M.S. in Library and Information Science from Simmons College, and a B.A. in English, Phi Beta Kappa, Magna Cum Laude from Brown University.

Jeremy Schlosberg is a freelance journalist who has written extensively on both technology and education for a wide variety of national publications, including *Good Housekeeping, Family Life, Home PC, Parenting, Smart Money,* and *Salon*.

Part One

An Introduction to Distance Learning

Chapter One

The Opportunities

How many times have you wished you could make time for that master's or doctorate degree you've always wanted? If only your life weren't so hectic, if only the college you would like to attend weren't so far away, if only your other responsibilities didn't limit the time you have to pursue an advanced degree. If only, if only.

It's time to put an end to "if only"—if only because it's beside the point nowadays. If you want to learn, there are plenty of options that can put a graduate degree in your hand without requiring you to quit your job, relocate, or otherwise reengineer your life or lifestyle. Once upon a time, the student had to go to where the education was. Today, increasingly often, the education will come to you.

This has a lot to do with that "wired" world you hear so much about. But being wired means far more than having cool stuff to look at on the World Wide Web: It means that information is no longer bound by place and time. You don't have to go to a library to look things up, and you don't have to go to a university to get a graduate degree. You can get one from your living room, your workplace, even your bedroom. The process by which this is done is called *distance learning.*

The idea of distance learning has been around for quite a while, but it hasn't always been considered a legitimate way to earn a degree. Even when the courses were good and the educational institutions offering them were trustworthy, the technology was limiting. After all, if a college decided to broadcast a course via closed-circuit TV, students still needed to travel to where TVs were set up to receive the broadcast, and be there at a specific time.

Computers have changed all that, thanks to the Internet. The Internet, too, has been around for a while, but it's been particularly friendly only since the early '90s. The advent of the World Wide Web has made it way easier than it used to be to find information on the Internet, which has caused many, many more people and institutions to put things there. What's more, the technological capacity of the average personal computer nowadays has allowed for sound and pictures to be distributed easily on the Web. The implications on the types and quality of courses that can be held online are only beginning to be felt.

In addition to the computer, other technology is coming into its own today that is generating a new era in distance learning. Videoconferencing in particular has made huge technological strides in recent years. There are many more colleges and universities delivering courses by satellite, cable, and broadcast television than ever before.

A Bit of History

Actually, the idea of putting a teacher or professor in front of a camera is not all that new. What we call distance learning today has its most direct roots in the emergence of closed-circuit television in the late 1950s. Closed-circuit TV was envisioned as a powerful solution for meeting educational and vocational training needs, especially for people in remote areas. West Virginia, of all places, was an early leader in supplying children as well as adults with programs delivered by closed circuit.

Although the delivery system (as people like to say in the distance-learning field) was new, education via television still depended upon traditional teaching methods—namely, the lecture and the blackboard. It was a natural enough idea, but the presentation looked static. In many cases, it was positively boring. This kind of mistake is common when new communication technologies are introduced: People will use them in old ways at first—ways that were not designed to take advantage of the newer technology's power. As a result, the new technologies don't seem very engaging after the novelty wears off.

So it's no surprise, really, that this first generation of TV-based distance learning didn't take the country by storm. There's no getting around the boredom of the one-way, "talking head" presentation. What's more, distance learning via television still required the student to watch the class at a predetermined time.

Earlier efforts at distance learning employed the simplest medium of them all: pen, paper, and postage stamps. Correspondence courses may not traditionally be the most reputable or trustworthy way of getting an education, but their popularity with generations of Americans (dating back to Benjamin Franklin) attests to the strength of our collective eagerness to learn and to find some way to fit that learning into our existing lives. The American tradition of the chautauqua is another such effort. Begun in the late 19th century as a sort of intellectual summer camp for adults, the chautauqua became a wonderful way to have a spirited, informal learning experience through lively discussion with talented people. The remnants of this tradition persist to this day in the "Renaissance" weekends that President Clinton is involved with once a year, where distinguished scientists, academics, and others gather to discuss the great issues of the day. While not distance learning in the sense that we mean it now, the chautauqua is, however, another way we've attempted to find education outside the traditional bounds of the college campus and, at least partially, on our own terms.

Distance = Closeness?

It's called "distance learning," but in practice, distance-learning practitioners do everything they can to foster a sense of closeness between instructor and student, whether the two are separated by a few rooms or a few thousand miles.

One of the interesting things about distance learning is how opportunities arise for interaction with faculty as well as with other students that may be far more personal and intense than what happens in a traditional classroom. This seems particularly true with online courses. Students who rarely speak up in class might find a powerful and articulate voice through their fingertips. For many, the virtual classroom seems much more comfortable for expressing alternative opinions or challenging the professor. For some, the screen wall presented by the computer monitor allows for more reflection time and less personal embarrassment.

Maybe we don't really mean "distance" at all. Researchers who look at different technologies in learning situations are beginning to prefer the term distributed education. Whatever the current phrase or jargon, there's no doubt that new technologies have brought both familiar and unfamiliar university-level educational experiences to the willing learner.

Pioneers in Distance Learning

For distance learning to be viable as a serious educational option, there had to be a way to combine television's ability to reach remote areas with a truer sense of interactivity and attention to the individual student. Among the most notable experiments in recent decades were the pioneering efforts of the Open University (OU) in the United Kingdom and Nova University in the United States.

The Open University

From its earliest days, broadcast television was envisioned as a source not only of entertainment but of education. In the United States, a program called Sunrise Semester brought college courses to those intrepid souls willing to turn their sets on at 6:00 A.M., listen to a lecture, and do the homework assignments. Viewers who did the work were able to receive college credit from the university offering the course. The United Kingdom took this idea to a new level with the creation of the Open University in 1969.

Developing the novel idea that students needn't be present in a specific building at a specific time to earn a real degree, the Open University offered a series of college courses via broadcast TV. The courses were creatively designed, expertly taught, and extremely well produced. The camera became an integral part of the learning process, often taking the at-home student out of the classroom and into the real world. Students, whether taking courses for credit or not, were always given personal attention by the faculty.

Attention to detail and informed use of technology met with great success: The Open University attracted millions of participants and taught them well. By any criteria, an Open University education now measures up to the standards of most prestigious, traditional colleges. As a result, distance learning is a road to improvement for families throughout the United Kingdom. Interestingly, though, the Open University is only beginning to experiment with limited use of the Internet; educators there are being cautious about straying from their successful technological model.

Nova University

A more recent example here in the United States is Nova University (now Nova Southeastern University). One of the first institutions to incorporate the computer in a distance learning environment, Nova has been offering courses and full degree programs that combine daily online work and interaction with face-to-face weekend meetings for more than 15 years. The early years employed a computer network based on the UNIX operating system (the same basic system that the Internet grew on). Despite the technological difficulties (UNIX is not easy to learn and operate), students were enthusiastic from the start. Faculty members, too, had to learn to adapt to this new form of education. Instead of the traditional idea of regular, weekly office hours, instructors found that their online students demanded daily attention. Even the idea of how papers were written and graded changed: Student work was constantly in progress, with papers submitted electronically and then resubmitted for regrading. Learning was collaborative, the teacher growing along with the taught.

Truth be told, Nova University was not embraced by the traditional academic world when it first went online. The years have proven the institution's foresight, however, and its reputation has grown accordingly. Universities that once ridiculed Nova are now incorporating its methods.

Today's Options

In recent years, the distance learning bandwagon has grown larger and larger. As new technologies have emerged, distance learning programs of various shapes and sizes have appeared at a wider and wider array of institutions. Whether these universities have been pulled in by the possibility of expanding their admissions or pushed in by sales pitches from zealous hardware manufacturers, the bottom line, for you, is unprecedented variety and quality. Today, even the most prestigious institutions are examining their distance-learning options.

As you begin to evaluate the field, you'll see everything—from schools offering a smattering of unrelated courses to institutions with entire degree programs available through some combination of satellite technology, videoconferencing, and online interaction. Corporations, too, use these methods for employee education and training (either in-house or from a selected university). A fair number of independent, for-profit educational organizations have also sprouted onto the distance learning landscape, delivering education through cable television and satellite. Some exist exclusively as online entities.

One of the most interesting developments in the field is the trend in which a number of autonomous universities band together to form a *consortium* (more than one of which are called *consortia*). It's the kind of stuffy word academics like to use, but it's also a pretty cool idea: students participating in a distance learning consortium can have access to a far wider range of resources and a higher quality of teaching than any one institution might offer on its own. Chapter 3 of this book will give an in-depth look at a group of these consortia.

One of the big debates among distance learning advocates has centered on the effectiveness of one-way versus two-way interaction. That is: Should the students be able simply to listen to and see the teacher (that's what we mean by *one-way*), or should the teacher also be able to listen to and see the students (that'd be *two-way*)? Technology has advanced since the early days of closed-circuit, talking-head professors. Allowing students to respond either by telephone, fax, or computer has been technologically possible for a number of years. One-way communication, however, especially when television is involved, is still common.

By now, many students have been exposed to both one-way and two-way distance learning classes. There are many who believe that good education is possible only with two-way communication, allowing the teacher to see the students. But there is actually no evidence to prove this. Just because the instructor cannot see her students, and just because the students cannot necessarily respond to her in real time does not mean the class is dull and unengaging. Many talented teachers are experimenting with distance-learning classroom styles and approaches that provoke activity as well as interactivity.

So far, distance learning "classroom" environments vary widely—from engineering courses that show little more than the back of a teacher's head and a writing surface to those that ask challenging questions of students, require activity at each student's site, and create debates among the viewing

Distance Learning, Corporate Style

Thanks in particular to technological advancements offered by audio and video teleconferencing companies, distance learning has taken off in the corporate world in the last five years. Corporations of all sizes and in all industries see distance learning as a key new way to provide important skills and information to employees who may work in any number of different locations. From almost zero in 1985, there are now more than 6,500 companies regularly using videoconferencing today (Source: Gartner Group, 1996).

Videoconferencing through telephone connection is far less expensive for the institution to produce and deliver than designing and producing a video program and sending it via satellite. The production value of most videoconferences is minimal. While the instructor must operate within some fairly restrictive parameters (no hand waving or abrupt motions, please!), there is an undeniable immediacy and excitement felt when learning goes directly to the desktop. All the current technologies have success stories.

audience. Everywhere, the race is on to find the best way for students to talk back to the faculty, either during or after class. Fax, e-mail, telephone-based audioconferencing, and small electronic machines that allow instant yes-no responses from students are some of the methods being used right now.

Why Do It?

The university of the 21st century is being born now, in the last years of the 20th century. This new institution offers limitless possibilities for learning from the best teachers and using top-notch resources, wherever you are and whenever you want. As distance learning advocates envision it, soon the greatest teachers in the world will be available to students in even the smallest, most remote areas. The student body in the 21st century university will be gloriously heterogeneous, giving learners extraordinary opportunities for interaction and electronic socialization. World peace will arrive.

Well, okay, maybe that last part is doubtful. And maybe the first part is, too. The truth is, no one really knows where all of this is going. But the fun part is that we don't have to know just yet. There is already great promise out there, and wonderful benefits waiting for those who take the time to scope out the distance-learning marketplace and see what's in it for them.

Regardless of exactly where the distance learning revolution takes us, there's no doubting that major educational change is in the air. The university is transforming itself from the sacrosanct purveyor of all learning to the collector and integrator of knowledge. The role of the student is bound to change in the process as well. No longer passive recipients of pronouncements from on high, students of the future will want and need to create their own meaning guided by those who have traveled the road before them, as well as by their fellow educational journeyers.

Perhaps the most significant change in students of the future will be in their demographic composition. It's begun to change already, but we are still, culturally, locked in to the idea that higher education is for the relatively young. And yet the American workplace of the present and the future all but demands otherwise. A recent study conducted by Washington State University surveyed over 1,000 working adults and demonstrated that most employees need additional learning or training every two years merely to maintain their present positions. If you're seeking to find a better job or more responsibility within your current job, then additional course work or even an advanced degree not only is important but might be essential. "Getting educated once is not enough in our knowledge-based society," the study concluded.

And yet the study also showed that as people grew older, they were increasingly unwilling to go to a college campus to learn. They were, however, responsive to the idea of alternative, technologically based educational methods.

And who can blame us? Enrolling in a graduate program can be extraordinarily inconvenient if you are already juggling job, home, and family. Most people simply can't manage it. Which means that distance learning may be the only way to provide personal and corporate growth—it is, perhaps, the definitive response to the long-standing barriers that have existed to the concept of lifelong learning.

At the same time, the concept of lifelong learning seems more vital than ever. In today's ever-changing marketplace, knowledge and skill sets become obsolete with alarming speed. There are many, in fact, who would like to scare you into believing that the workplace of the near future will be a relentlessly Darwinian jungle in which those who don't stay constantly educated will be brutally downsized. This may be an extremist vision. On the other hand, let's just say it may not be such a bad thing that continued education is getting easier and easier to access.

So if you need more education to be promoted and you need to find the most efficient strategy, perhaps you should try a technological solution. If you don't like what you're doing, if you're feeling drained and dispirited by your daily routine, maybe it's time to try something different. Among further benefits, distance learning brings new opportunities for adventure. For the lonely, there are easy companionships, with both the teaching faculty and fellow students. A kind of esprit de corps develops among distance learners that is rarely found among adults who meet once a week in a classroom seminar or lecture hall.

That's why you might do it. Why do it now? Well, you'll have to be the judge of how much the distance-learning solution for graduate education fits in with your sense of life and sense of self. But in the world of education, the time is ripe. More than ever before, there are legitimate institutions and reputable organizations involved in teaching far-flung students. A confluence of technologies has created great opportunity, and it sure is convenient.

Chapter Two

Promises and Pitfalls

So you've decided you're really going to do it—take a graduate program without setting foot in an actual classroom. This is sure to be exciting, but it might also be frustrating sometimes. After all, distance learning is still in its infancy, and just about everyone involved is still discovering how to make it all work. From your point of view as a student, getting started is not quite as straightforward as applying to a traditional university. This isn't about just filling out an application form and making some obvious comparisons. You need to be a smart consumer and get the answers to a number of important questions in advance—questions about technology, quality, and how a particular program fits in with your personal needs and lifestyle.

Choosing a distance-learning program is a personal decision—even more so than choosing a traditional higher-education program. To make a successful choice, you must select a program that fits into your existing, and probably long-established, lifestyle. And we're not talking about just a month or two: If you are starting a full graduate program, it will take several years , possibly longer. That's a good reason for taking a bit of extra time now to be sure you're making the best choice possible.

Technology Choices

Colleges and universities today employ many different technologies—or, remember, delivery systems—to put their distance-learning programs in place. Some deliver the courses directly to your home, while others might require use of your company's facilities, and still others might require you to go to an alternative location.

The following summary is a quick introduction to what's out there with a few words about each technology's strengths and weaknesses from the student's point of view. We've separated the technologies to help you understand each one better, but bear in mind that many programs will combine these technologies—for instance, a course delivered via cable television may also use an online connection to allow individual work with faculty and with fellow students.

As you read through this, begin to picture yourself involved in whatever learning environment is described. See how it sounds and feels to you. This is part of the personal nature of the decision. Some people will be more comfortable with certain of the technological options than others. Keep an open mind, but don't deny your gut reactions either.

Audioconferencing

How it works: Students are gathered around a table with an audio device that is also a telephone. They listen to instruction through the device, and hold discussions both among themselves and with the instructor. Students often receive audiocassettes to supplement the audioconference.

Strength: Reasonable cost for the institution, meaning a less expensive class for you.

Weaknesses: Can be difficult to concentrate on for long periods; requires attendance at a specific time in a specific location.

Audiographics

How it works: Like audioconferencing, students are gathered around a table with a telephone. Here, however, there is additional piece of equipment that can display graphics, functioning more or less as a remote chalkboard.

Strengths: Reasonable cost plus some visual reinforcement.

Weaknesses: Still largely sound based; requires attendance at a specific time in a specific location.

Broadcast Television

How it works: College courses are broadcast locally or regionally via public television. Many are supported by additional reading material and/or videos.

Strengths: Accessible from the home; opportunity exists for great visual excitement, through both quality production techniques and teaching locations beyond the classroom; students can videotape the programs for later review.

Weaknesses: Largely talking-head style instruction, which means that instructors must have a highly engaging personality to overcome student boredom; requires self-discipline to stick with it.

Cable Television

How it works: Local access cable television channels often fill time with educational programs operated directly by local school systems, colleges, and universities.

Strengths: Same as broadcast television. There is at least one national educational entity, Jones Education Company (JEC), which offers both undergraduate and graduate degrees via cable TV (see chapter 3).

Weaknesses: Same as broadcast television; plus, cable is not only less widely accessible than broadcast, but local cable offerings are inconsistent to the point that channels you want may not be available to you.

Computer Courses

How it works: It varies. Sometimes courses are offered on CD-ROM, with all of the course content in one neat package—similar to a text-based series, with visual material built in either as slide images or snippets of video. Other computer courses are offered via the Internet, which means that you must have a computer with a modem. Interaction with the instructor takes place via e-mail.

Strengths: Extreme convenience if you own a computer; also has the potential for meaningful, one-to-one interaction with the faculty as well as online chat sessions with fellow students.

Weaknesses: If the program isn't CD-ROM based, you will need to be comfortable with going online, downloading material onto your computer, and spending many hours at the screen; requires commitment from faculty to spend time online too, which may or may not happen.

Satellite Courses

How it works: A class is taught before a camera in a remote studio, and the video feed is transmitted to one of the many communications satellites orbiting the earth. The satellite then retransmits the signal to a "downlink" receiver dish on the roof of a facility where students are assembled to watch and take part in the class. Often, a special "audiobridge" telephone connection allows faculty and students to communicate if the course is being watched in "real time"—that is, as the instructor is actually teaching it.

Strengths: A popular method for receiving education at both corporate and alternative-campus locations; students can see their instructor, who is usually more aware of the specific audience for the course than a broadcast or cable TV instructor. Classes can be videotaped and reviewed at leisure.

Weaknesses: Dependent on fixed locations for student and faculty; the potential for compatibility problems between the studio transmitting the course and the building that is attempting to receive it (because satellite technology is currently in the middle of switching from analog to digital transmission); also, the telephone connection allowing interaction with the faculty is limited, in that not everyone who wants to talk gets the chance.

Videoconferencing

How it works: Equipment uses telephone lines to transmit video images to desktop computer systems, so that everyone involved can be seen and heard. Videoconference systems can either be room based (so that the students gather as a group to be seen and heard by the instructor) or desktop based (so that individual students have their own systems).

Strengths: Inexpensive compared to satellite time, and relatively easy to set up between a small number of locations; class meets in real time and allows visual and vocal interaction between instructor and students; no special studios are required at the instructor's end.

Weaknesses: Special equipment is required; more likely to be dependent on a fixed location than online learning. While computer manufacturers anticipate offering built-in videoconferencing in standard PCs in the near future, such systems will not be common for many years; and, for good picture quality, you need not one but three ISDN telephone lines.

Videotape Delivery

How it works: Classes are recorded on video and sent directly to students for viewing at home.

Strengths: Location independent and time independent; student can view entirely at his convenience, and review for comprehension as many times as necessary.

Weaknesses: Production quality varies tremendously—some videos show only dull, talking heads, while others have Hollywood-style glitz and pizzazz (which isn't always a positive, either); plus the lack of built-in opportunity for interaction with either the instructor or fellow students.

There, that wasn't so complicated, was it? It's worth noting that all these technologies are continuing to become more user-friendly as well as more often used in combination with one another. Most worthwhile distance learning programs actively seek ways to make things more personal and more accommodating to the individual learner. That's you.

What's Quality and What's Not

Unfortunately for all of us, there's no Good Housekeeping Seal of Approval for distance-learning programs. In this relatively new and continually changing field, there are few sure things. We can't guarantee you a great program and a successful next few years. What we can do, however, is point you in the right direction, and give you the information you need to help you make your own decisions.

To begin your search, check the list of degree programs that comprises the heart of this book. Instead of giving you a comprehensive list of every available graduate-level, distance-learning program offered anywhere on the planet, we offer a selective list of programs, culled with quality in mind from a variety of sources, including recommendations of students we have met at meetings and conferences on distance learning, the award-winning entries of an annual contest sponsored by the United States Distance Learning Association (USDLA), extensive telephone conversations, the Internet, and a wide variety of articles on the subject. Among the programs listed are many offered by prestigious universities, well-known colleges, and other organizations that have been in this business for a while. Some programs we discuss are offered by newcomers, and one group mentioned here (Western Governors Virtual University) has yet to run its first course.

Every quality degree program is bound to have its share of great courses, and perhaps a few duds. Once you enroll in a program, it's up to you to find out who the extraordinary professors are and identify the best courses, as you would at any college. But in a distance-learning situation, there is some additional information you can look for to help you both scope out a program in advance and keep an eye on things once you're in it.

Look at the Numbers—and Behind Them

Begin your investigation with a series of quantitative questions; the answers to these should be relatively easy to gather.

- How many courses does the institution offer?
- Does the institution specialize in your particular area of interest?
- How many years has the program been running?
- How many faculty are teaching in the program?
- How much training do teachers get, if any?
- How many students are in a class?
- How often is it necessary to participate actively?
- What is the dropout rate?
- How long is each session?
- How many credits do you need for a degree?
- How much does it cost?

Okay, that's a lot of questions. Fortunately, we've answered them for you in this book, at least regarding the programs we've selected. But on the one hand, it's worth having these questions in mind should you be in the position of attempting to evaluate a new or different program at some point. And on the other hand, this evaluation process isn't just about asking questions; it's also about interpreting answers. Here's a bit of help on that score.

Track Record and Courses

Just as you gravitate towards doctors or hospitals with track records for providing outstanding medical care, you might want to look at those institutions that have been around for a while, offer large numbers of courses (especially in your area of interest), and feature a rich assortment of faculty. A good sign of a quality program is that faculty members have taught the same distance-learning course a few different times: Teaching via technology is a new skill, and instructors get better at it with experience.

On the other hand, it is possible, though not likely, for a school to make all of its courses "distance learning" courses by putting a camera in the classroom, connecting to a satellite uplink or to cable TV, and beginning wholesale transmission. A lot of courses and teachers are involved, but you don't necessarily get a committed distance-learning effort. In fact, sometimes you get something pretty awful.

How bad can it get? Some teachers are terrified of teaching in front of a camera and literally try to hide. Others possess a teaching style that is hopelessly dreary when filmed (such as those engineering professors—they know who they are—who teach by reading what they write on a white board, as they write it). Others simply can't deal with a teaching situation that doesn't guarantee their 50 minutes of lecture time; to such instructors, the idea of answering students' questions—especially faceless questions from remote locations—is abhorrent. It keeps them from covering all their material.

We once heard how an associate started a distance-learning operation at a state college by telling faculty members that they needn't do anything different from their ordinary teaching. He lied, assuring everyone that they could teach as they always had because it was doubtful they would teach otherwise. These teachers quickly learned this wasn't true, but fortunately they were all capable of change and did a good job. This may be an extreme case, but remember that faculty have to pay attention to you, the remote learner. And they absolutely must understand their curriculum in this new context. The most effective distance-learning programs conscientiously train faculty for their new roles.

Number of Students

How many in a class is important, partially for obvious enough reasons. Too many students and individual attention will be all but impossible for the instructor to manage; likewise will it be difficult for you, the student, to participate actively and regularly, if that's what you'd like to do. There may be something wrong with having too few students also, however—it could be a sign of a program without purpose or commitment, and could indicate some lack of teaching quality. It also limits the potential for interaction with your fellow distance learners. Then again, a small class could be an amazing opportunity to study closely with a talented professor.

So look behind the numbers. If the class is large, perhaps there are teaching assistants (TAs) who are knowledgeable and available to answer questions. If the class is small, perhaps the professor is still wonderful. Remember above all that the more you become involved by knowing the professor, by communicating with fellow classmates, and by speaking up in whatever format is available for you, the more likely you are to stay the course.

This becomes an important consideration for you in advance. One of the biggest problems with learning from home is the possible isolation and need for self-discipline. All institutions involved with teaching through these new technologies are concerned about dropout rates. A high rate could be a red flag about a questionable program.

Session Length

When it comes to a program's time frame, distance learning changes the game a little bit. A course that might take fifteen weeks when taught traditionally might well take as little as six to ten hours in a distance-learning environment. Sometimes the added visual elements—for instance, illustrating a topic through a minidrama rather than paragraphs in a textbook—speed up the learning process. So you are not getting shortchanged if a course seems to be quicker through technology. That's one of the benefits.

Cost

Lots of people assume you get what you pay for. But this isn't always true. The range of costs for distance-learning courses is very similar to the range for traditional college graduate programs. Your best guiding principle is to look for the kind of institutional costs you would have chosen for a traditional campus setting. Now, freed from geographic boundaries, you have lots more options in your price range.

You should know from the outset that financial aid is generally not available for distance-learning courses. Much federal controversy surrounds this issue. Maybe something will happen someday, but in the meantime, our advice is: Plan to pay for the whole program. If you find that federal or state loans are possible, consider it an unexpected bonus. If your education is partially or wholly work motivated, you might find your company willing to pay for at least part of the sum.

As with a traditional, campus-based education, be sure that when you're figuring out the cost, you add up absolutely everything that will have to be paid for, including books, fees, and other incidentals. If you'll need to travel regularly or occasionally either to the campus or to an alternative central location, throw in your travel expenses too. Create, in advance, as precise an annual cost figure as possible.

Read Between the Lines

Information about colleges and universities from the institutions themselves is factual, but not necessarily revealing. There are ways, however, of looking at some of the standard information with a discriminating eye; learning to read between the lines can help you understand more about a program than the description was intended to reveal.

Accreditation

The first thing to look for is whether the school that interests you has been accredited by a regional accrediting agency. While there can be reasons that reputable institutions have yet to be accredited—because, for instance, they are so new, and accreditation takes time (typically 2 to 5 years)—be sure to look long and hard at any educational entity that lacks accreditation.

There are many different accrediting agencies for schools and colleges. The most prestigious are the regional agencies (see the sidebar listing on the next page). Here the process is most rigorous, including a self-study, site visit, and careful consideration of inadequacies. What's more, some of the agencies are even more careful about course and degree programs involving remote locations and technological delivery systems.

Understand that even institutions that have long been accredited still have to apply to the state for an authorization to add new or distance-learning programs to the school's offerings. This alone can take six months or more, and may require a site visit by a team of peers. In a field as new and constantly changing as distance learning, this will no doubt mean that many fine programs still lack an official stamp of recognition. Most are in the process, however, so you might be wary of a program that can't at least report on where it is in the accreditation process.

Technology

You can gain insight into a program by examining the underlying technology in a bit of detail. How current or outmoded is it? Most important, do your best to determine that the technology you will use in the program will be around for the length of the program. If not, you'll be dealing with a potentially frustrating upgrade situation. Wherever you receive your courses must be capable and willing to change if the delivery system is upgraded; this includes your own house.

Of course, technological progress is an ongoing wild card. Take the cable modem, which is destined, before long, to become a major delivery system in its own right. A cable modem essentially lets you use your TV set like a

Accreditation Agencies

Unlike most other countries in the world, the United States lacks a centralized authority to oversee postsecondary education. While the individual states do exert a certain amount of control over education in general, for the most part, our colleges and universities are allowed to operate with great independence.

At some level, however, we need to know that certain quality standards are maintained. For this knowledge, we have come to rely upon a group of voluntary, nongovernmental membership associations to attest to the quality of our post-secondary educational institutions. These associations are known as accreditation agencies.

Most standard accreditation is handled by a lineup of six regional agencies, each of which is a voluntary, nonprofit, self-governing entity. Each has adopted criteria by which to judge the quality of an educational program along with procedures for evaluating whether individual institutions or programs are living up to these standards. In addition to these regional agencies, there are a wide range of nationally oriented accreditation agencies which focus on specialized areas of knowledge, in areas such as health, theology, and the arts. These specialized agencies may offer accreditation for either a specific program within a larger institution, or for an entire institution if the institution itself is specialized in the one area.

Some of the regional accreditation agencies mentioned in this book are:

Middle States Association of Colleges and Schools

New England Association of Schools and Colleges

North Central Association of Colleges and Schools

Northwest Association of Schools and Colleges

Southern Association of Colleges and Schools

Western Association of Schools and College

Some of the specialized accreditation agencies you will see in the listings are:

Accrediting Board for Engineering and Technology

American Assembly of Collegiate Schools of Business

American Council on Pharmaceutical Education

Computer Science Accrediting Board

National League for Nursing

computer. You'll notice it wasn't listed in our group of delivery systems, because there isn't a college or educational institution using cable modems yet. But bet your boots that what is today available through your computer in the way of Internet courses will be accessed also by cable modems in the near future.

Library Issues

Be sure to investigate what kind of library facilities you will have. The college library may be essential to your course of study. Can it be accessed electronically? Understand that online access does not mean access to every word contained in every book in the library's collection; it can mean, however, both access to the electronic card catalog and, potentially, full-text access to some or all of the library's magazines, journals, and newspapers. This can be extremely helpful, especially considering the widespread trend among graduate schools for periodical- rather than book-oriented collections.

In any case, unless all print material is sent through the mails, by fax, or online, you will need to find stuff either through the college library, your local library, or the Internet. It's important to know the details of your resource needs and options in advance.

Faculty Issues

Questions about faculty are vital. In some of the most prestigious institutions, faculty have shunned remote teaching assignments like the plague. They have built their institutional credibility on lecturing, researching, and writing. Technology puts far more emphasis on teaching methods and interpersonal skills. Interestingly, this bothers some professors. After all, responding to individual students interrupts the flow, and often does not allow the professors to cover all of the planned material. Instructors need to be at once more tightly prepared and more willing to go with the flow. And when it comes to a presentation before the camera, they need a far greater awareness than most intuitively have of what makes for a compelling visual presentation.

What's more, student interaction is legitimately time-consuming. any faculty members expected to teach twenty students—but with remote learners find themselves teaching a class of 100 or more. They do not receive extra compensation, relief from other duties, additional status, or any perks for a great deal of extra effort. For untenured faculty, the situation is downright dispiriting, for they normally receive no credit or recognition for distance-learning work, no publication credits for their electronic writings. So it is as though this part of their academic life is purely voluntary.

The bottom line for you is to ascertain to the best of your ability that the institution you choose has a cadre of faculty who accept the challenge of remote students eagerly, with support from their institution.

Does the Shoe Fit?

Let's think a little about your comfort level before you begin your selection process. If you are not genuinely ready for the degree program that you choose, you'll spend time and money and probably never finish. Remember that dropout rate!

Begin with this simple question: Are you comfortable with technology? Not only technology in general, but the technology involved in distance learning in particular. Will a pure audio program be something you can live with? Can you adapt to the slight delay in interaction that happens with many videoconferencing systems, or will that little but noticeable out-of-sync factor between seeing the lips move and hearing the words drive you nuts?

If you're thinking about television-based courses, picture the environment carefully. Will the lack of immediate response in broadcast, or the queues for satellite questions frustrate you?

And as the world rushes online, you'd better stop and examine your own, personal attitudes towards the ubiquitous computer. Are you comfortable there? Are you used to getting on the Internet, and all the little delays that can involve? Are you excited by downloading information or mystified by the process? Your response to these and related questions may tell you what kind of technology delivery system to be looking for.

One question not to overlook is the convenience issue. How convenient is the convenience of the distance-learning programs you're considering? As we've seen, while all deliver education to places that are not the campus, not all of them deliver directly to your home. Make sure you really have time for and don't mind the trips that might be required to attend the classes. And don't forget the real-time factor. Unless courses are completely computer- and/or video-oriented, there are going to be actual classes happening at specific times that you will have to be free to "attend," even if it's rom your own home on your own television. Carefully relate the course schedule to your personal schedule. Do the times and days match your availability? Don't make light of occasional conflicts. Nothing will end a program faster than realizing you'll be "on the road" even once a month for the duration of the course. It's far too easy to slip behind to the point that you simply can't continue.

Beyond those things related specifically to the distance-learning aspect of this type of education, there are other issues to consider—issues that prospective students have always had to mull over before applying for a degree program. Okay, the time-honored urban campus versus rural campus debate is irrelevant in the distance learning milieu, but other traditional questions remain. What kind of school do you really want? What sort of academic atmosphere do you enjoy? Look at the admissions requirements. Is the school likely to be filled with highly competitive students, or flagrantly laid-back ones? Sometimes you can tell this by the description of the school and what they expect of students. In which environment will you be happiest? One thing you might try to do to help you get an insider's view of any program you're seriously considering is ask to talk to someone who has already been through it.

Sure, we're asking you to think through a lot of things. But this is a major commitment of time, effort, and money we're talking about. Make the best decision you can up front and you will benefit many times over in the years to come. To help you get started on this decision, try taking the following quiz.

Are Telecourses for You? A Self-Quiz

This quiz was developed by the Northern Virginia Community College's Extended Learning Institute to help prospective students assess how well a distance-learning program would fit their circumstances and lifestyles. Choose one answer for each question and then check the score explanations at the end.

1. My need to take this course now is:

❐ A. High. I need it immediately for a degree, job, or other important reason.

❐ B. Moderate. I could take it on campus later or substitute another course.

❐ C. Low. It's a personal interest that could be postponed.

2. Feeling that I am part of a class is:

❐ A. Not particularly necessary for me.

❐ B. Somewhat important to me.

❐ C. Very important to me.

3. I would classify myself as someone who:

❐ A. Often gets things done ahead of time.

❐ B. Needs reminding to get things done on time.

❐ C. Puts things off until the last minute.

4. Classroom discussion is:

❐ A. Rarely helpful to me.

❐ B. Sometimes helpful to me.

❐ C. Almost always helpful to me.

5. When an instructor hands out directions for an assignment, I prefer:

❐ A. Figuring out the instructions myself.

❐ B. Trying to follow the directions on my own, then asking for help as needed.

❐ C. Having the directions explained to me.

6. I need faculty comments on my assignments:

❐ A. Within a few weeks, so I can review what I did.

❐ B. Within a few days, or I forget what I did.

❐ C. Right away or I get frustrated.

7. Considering my professional and personal schedule, the amount of time I have to work on a telecourse is:

❐ A. More than enough for a campus class or a telecourse.

❐ B. The same as for a class on campus.

❐ C. Less than for a class on campus.

8. When I am asked to use VCRs, computers, voice mail, or other technologies new to me:

❐ A. I look forward to learning new skills.

❐ B. I feel apprehensive, but try it anyway.

❐ C. I put it off or try to avoid it.

9. As a reader, I would classify myself as:

❐ A. Good. I usually understand the text without help.

❐ B. Average. I sometimes need help to understand the text.

❐ C. Slower than average.

10. If I have to go to campus to take exams or complete work:

❐ A. I can go to campus anytime.

❐ B. I may miss some lab assignments or exam deadlines if campus labs are not open evenings and weekends.

❐ C. I will have difficulty getting to the campus, even in the evenings and on weekends.

Scoring

Give yourself three points for each A that you chose, two points for each B, and one point for each C. If you scored between 24 and 30, distance learning is a real possibility for you. If you scored between 17 and 23, distance learning may work for you, but you may need to make a few adjustments to your schedule or habits to succeed. If you scored between 10 and 16, distance learning may not be a suitable option for you right now.

Part Two

The
Programs

Chapter Three

Large Organizations and Consortia

One group of distance-learning organizations plays in a larger league than everyone else. The organizations within this group are all different and quite complex; one thing they have in common, however, is that each is a consortium—that is, each of these "big league" organizations works in collaboration with its member universities.

These consortia didn't get big overnight: The organizations listed here are not only some of the largest distance-learning efforts that exist today, but are also, with one exception, some of the most well-established. Whether or not you end up deciding to enter the world of distance learning through a consortium's gates, it's worth your while to know a thing or two about them—why they exist, what they do, and how they do it.

While the organizations chosen for this chapter are not the only distance-learning consortia in existence, they represent the cream of the crop—outfits that deliver top-quality learning. Together, they demonstrate that a "collective" can be a responsible and effective source of educational programs, using many technologies and different delivery systems. Each may provide reasonable choices to assist you in making a decision.

For more specific information about these organizations and the programs they offer, see their listings in chapter 4.

The Organizations

A*DEC

A*DEC is a new name for an organization formerly known as Agsat, a non-profit consortium of about 50 colleges and universities, that began by delivering satellite courses to students at agricultural colleges. This was a new way of sharing resources and expertise, and it brought the world of agricultural education together. The courses were developed by many top-quality, land-grant colleges and universities. The Land Grant Act of 1862 laid the foundation for agriculturally oriented institutions throughout the country to conduct research, extension, and teaching, available not only to on-campus students but to any resident of the institution's state. Agsat's pioneering satellite courses laid the groundwork for an organization that has become a distance-learning champion.

You might say that A*DEC today is inventing the idea of a "global land grant"—an opportunity to bring practical education to a worldwide constituency. The organization and its representative universities have also been in the forefront of each new technological advance. They were among the first to attempt "learning on demand" for students of agriculture and related fields by introducing a continuous broadcast—all day, all night—on several channels. (Several cable companies are now testing this kind of distribution with movies, calling it "almost on demand.") A*DEC will most probably be among the leaders in offering digital satellite transmission on a large scale.

A*DEC's member institutions (see the sidebar on the next page for a complete listing) provide all the courses and other learning-related programs for the group, making A*DEC istelf a "virtual organization." It has only three staffers to coordinate hundreds of courses, many hundreds of faculty, and an incredible array of learning opportunities. At the backbone of this effort is A*DEC's electronic network—a nationwide system containing 39 uplinks and more than 2,000 downlinks (a satellite system works with an uplink to send programs up to the satellite orbiting above and around us, and a series of downlinks to bring the signal down into a school, workplace, or home). This allows A*DEC to broadcast programs from 39 colleges to more than 2,000 schools and businesses. Be impressed—this is a big operation.

In fact, this network is impressive enough to have attracted many partner organizations that have no direct connection to college or graduate education. These partners are primarily interested in the gathering and disseminating of information, and include a wide assortment of government agencies and a good number of science- and technology-oriented foundations and associations. The government partnerships have brought money for developing good programming and databases, and have facilitated the dissemination of the latest research throughout the A*DEC community. For these reasons, A*DEC students always have a wide range of important information at their fingertips. Want to know about the new telecommunications bill, corn prices, or the effects of lunar exploration upon the environment? Look at the news and information sources on A*DEC's Information network. A*DEC's partners often find working with A*DEC an

A*DEC LAND GRANT MEMBERS

Alcorn State University

Clemson University

Colorado State University

Cornell University

Delaware State University

Florida A&M University

Iowa State University

Kansas State University

Mississippi State University

New Mexico State University

North Carolina A&T University

North Carolina State University

Ohio State University

Oklahoma State University

Oregon State University

Pennsylvania State University

Purdue University

Rutgers University

South Dakota State University

Tennessee State University

Texas A&M University

Tuskegee University

University of Arizona

University of Arkansas

University of Arkansas at Pine Bluff

University of California

University of Delaware

University of Florida

University of Georgia

University of Idaho

University of Illinois

University of Kentucky

University of Maine

University of Maryland—College Park

University of Maryland—Eastern Shore

University of Minnesota

University of Missouri at Columbia

University of Nebraska—Lincoln

University of Nevada—Reno

University of New Hampshire

University of Tennessee

University of Wisconsin

University of Wyoming

Utah State University

Virginia Polytechnic Institute and State University

Washington State University

West Virginia University

effective way of getting information to various audiences—the way, for instance, the National Science Foundation recently held a successful series of programs for researchers through the A*DEC network.

From elected officials to business executives, from elementary school teachers to community agency leaders, all sorts of people with computers use information that is both researched and distributed by A*DEC member institutions through the network. Subject areas have expanded beyond the primary interest of food and agriculture into related topics such as nutrition, health, and environmental studies, as well as into economic development and family-related issues. The information is available to the public in a number of ways—through courses, workshops, seminars, satellite discussion groups, online round tables, and more. Technologies used include the Internet, satellite, videotape, and audioconferences, often in combination with one another.

Above all, perhaps, think of A*DEC as a vast information resource. All of A*DEC's colleges and students rely upon it to keep them informed about developments that affect their interests. When you sign up at one of the A*DEC institutions, you have access to their online database and information services. Anyone interested in distance learning can benefit from the mind-boggling range of material on the consortium's well-kept Web page (www.adec.edu), which includes in-depth articles and well-researched links. There is even a sample course on the Web site for you to try out. UCLA Extension, University of Nebraska, Iowa State University, and Cornell University, among others, offer courses and seminars through the A*DEC structure. Although there is only one graduate degree offered by participating universities through A*DEC so far, many of these universities offer graduate degrees via distance learning outside of the A*DEC umbrella. You can expect more graduate degrees to be offered directly through A*DEC in the future.

In the meantime, the organization is doing ground-breaking work in researching questions about both licensing and intellectual property rights that are troubling for all distance-learning operations. For example, when a faculty member creates a course, does it belong to that person or to the institution? Can the college lease the rights to the course to other colleges? What happens when the course is created by or used through a consortium? Issues such as these are very important to anyone interested in seeing distance learning develop into a vital part of our educational future. Transferability of courses from one state to another, not to mention from one country to another, is another critical issue if distance learning is going to become a mainstream educational reality. A*DEC gives small grants to its member institutions for research in areas of mutual interest.

One thing seems clear: The efforts of organizations like A*DEC are hastening that day. With collaboration, partnerships, and joint governance, many of the A*DEC universities are beginning to accept each others' offerings; they also enjoy using A*DEC's small grants to research common problems and to evaluate offerings. Both of these developments are good news for you, the potential distance-learning consumer. Keep your eye on this ongoing success story.

The Jones Education Company

Glenn R. Jones is one of distance learning's true visionaries. His dream child, Mind Extension University (MEU), founded in the 1970s, used cable television to bring hundreds of courses and degree programs from dozens of universities to students in their living rooms. MEU was nothing if not well planned and enthusiastically supported. Perhaps the courses overused the static lecture format, but students almost always gave the organization high marks for educational effectiveness in the surveys that MEU frequently conducted.

But Mind Extension University is no more. Although Jones loved the school's name, people often characterized it as something out of the psychedelic '60s. Eventually, as the field and his company expanded, Jones recognized the need for a new name to complement the new structure. So he organized the original cable courses into a new department called The College Connection, which now offers undergraduate and graduate degrees from a dozen different colleges.

The range of offerings is broad and varied. On the graduate level, there are three whole programs: a Master of Arts in business communications directly from International University that focuses on both the business applications and the human factors relating to today's communications technology, a Master of Education in education technology leadership from George Washington University (based on the highly regarded MEU program which preceded it), and a Master of Business Administration from the University of Colorado at Colorado Springs. Courses leading to a graduate degree in Health Administration from Governors State University are now part of the overall program. Coming soon will be a Master of Science in Nursing from California State University at Dominguez Hills.

Another new branch of the Jones organization is Knowledge TV: A 24-hour-a-day series of classes and courses dedicated to, as company literature puts it, "practical, personal, and professional enrichment of its viewers." It is delivered via cable (if your cable company carries it) and satellite (if you have a satellite dish) to millions of viewers in the United States and around the world. A daily offering might include such courses as "Principles of Accounting II" or "Introduction to the Hospitality Industry" or informational programs such as "AIDS Unmasked: New Treatments, New Hopes."

The latest company born of Jones Education is International University College, which delivers courses produced by either itself or by other collegiate sources, primarily over the Internet. Its initial master's program, a Master of Arts in business communications developed in-house, has more than 30 courses, all delivered over the Internet and the World Wide Web. While the College Connection has a video base through cable, International University College uses little video beyond short QuickTime™ clips on the Internet. In fact, they assert that students don't want much video because it slows down the computer and makes the lessons take longer to complete.

International University College recently publicized its first graduate, a woman who started the course work in the spring of 1995 from a remote community in Colorado while simultaneously working a 60-hour week. The College is seeking accreditation from the North Central Association (NCA) of Colleges and Schools, one of five United States regional accreditation agencies. As we've already discussed, regional accreditation is a difficult and rigorous process. In March 1997, International was accepted for candidacy by the NCA; those who know about the accreditation process say this is pretty much the same as being accredited. Still, International University College must achieve full accreditation within five years or lose its candidacy.

The advantage of an organization like Jones is the outside support and administrative structure they provide. Registration is easy. Resource materials sent from the bookstore arrive on time—a major source of frustration in many other programs. This is not a neophyte organization starting a distance-learning network by trial and error but an experienced cadre of people who know what they're doing. The partner institutions are reputable colleges and universities. Jones the visionary has also proved himself to be a savvy businessperson; he's built a solid organization around him, and he knows how to listen to his constituency. If your area of interest or need overlaps with the material Jones offers, you should investigate further.

PBS Adult Learning Service

One of the most respected learning organizations in the nation is the Public Broadcasting System (PBS). In 1981, Ambassador Walter Annenberg gave $150 million to the Corporation for Public Broadcasting to create university telecourses in a variety of media. The money has gone in a number of directions, but one of the notable efforts it inspired was the Adult Learning Service (ALS).

ALS is comprised of three segments. First is (watch out, another unpronounceable acronym!) the Adult Learning Satellite Service, or ALSS. PBS promotes this as "the nation's largest satellite service for higher education," which is difficult to verify but it's pretty darned big. Second is Ready to

Earn, which offers workforce education through a variety of services including satellite, print, and on-site relationships. The third part of ALS is called Going the Distance, which offers two-year degrees by satellite and Internet.

ALSS comprises the largest part of ALS, offering high-quality courses to colleges, universities, and libraries. Produced in large part with the Annenberg cash, ALSS courses are most often created in local settings by a broad spectrum of noteworthy institutions, including Harvard University, Penn State University, and the Smithsonian. These programs are then shown on satellite at specific times, arranged by PBS with the colleges. Interested students go to special rooms for viewing. The entities that produce the programs may also license the programs to be taped and used beyond the classroom. The PBS Web page (www.pbs.org) allows a prospective student to see which institutions use ALSS courses, along with the chance to try out a sample course.

While PBS itself offers no degrees, distance learning is essential to the institutions they serve. Basically, any college or university in the country can pay to have PBS courses sent to the campus. Many community colleges across the country rely upon these courses for content material they can't handle locally. Other institutions, from Arizona State to the University of Wisconsin, use programs and courses as special events or curriculum offerings. While PBS produces some of its own programming, it also purchases telecourses from fine production houses and universities around the world.

If you find a PBS-produced distance-learning course you're interested in, you must meet the admissions criteria of the individual college or university offering it. Within its program, those that offer PBS telecourses will assign to the course a faculty member who will correspond with students on the Internet, grade papers, and give exams. Students form workgroups for continued communications. Textbooks are also sometimes uploaded and downloaded online.

The part of ALS known as Going the Distance (GTD) is a recent extension of the PBS distance learning effort. GTD allows 140 small colleges around the country to offer complete associate's degrees from a distance. Penn State University is evaluating the program and so far reports are good—the courses are better than expected, and the participating colleges are benefiting from being part of the distance-learning scene. This is not a graduate-level program, true, but the implications are significant for distance-learning efforts of all kinds. GTD targets adult learners in general, with a particular focus on people normally underserved by traditional campuses because of age, geographic location, or economic status. If GTD succeeds, it bodes well for higher-level distance-learning programs in the future.

The three primary areas for all PBS telecourses are science and math, education, and liberal arts. There are now several hundred individual courses and series in the ALSS library by now, and a catalog is sent out to thousands of institutions with the entire current library and some dates. Others can be accessed by borrowing or purchasing the tapes. The work is uniformly excellent, from production characteristics to the quality of the research and presentation. These programs were produced to reach the public, with a great deal more care and expense than courses for a classroom. What's more, many of the programs are not instructor-dependent—that is, the local professor who works with the students via the Internet is not the one who actually teaches the material.

As of now, ALS suffers from one major deficiency: It does not offer a whole degree program. Most of the courses were designed for other purposes, such as television specials, and need reshaping by the local institution. Many of them have been used as part of graduate-level courses and programs. Some, developed with Annenberg money specifically for university teaching, are extremely useful in a graduate program to plug in curriculum gaps. Certainly there are superb individual programs; some, too, are in series. But even among the series, few cover material in such a way as to equal a semester of instruction.

That said, understand that PBS is extremely interested in the growth of ALSS and all of its adult learning services. They have the hard part done already—that is, they have the satellites, the uplinks and downlinks, and the licensing agreements with all the colleges. Now they're ready to take that infrastructure and dramatically increase the offerings. More and more of ALS's new programs and alliances demonstrate this intent. In a recent interview, senior vice president of PBS Learning Services Jinny Goldstein talks about the many partnerships that ALSS already has, the three-and-one-half million students that have enrolled in PBS telecourses to date, and particularly the present and future uses of technology. Far from being an institution that was solely concerned with broadcast television, PBS now encompasses many formats and technologies.

PBS is a national treasure. Watch for its telecourses, seminars, and online offerings in the institution that you choose.

National Technological University (NTU)

Great organizations are often the result of great vision and leadership. Lionel Baldwin, the President of NTU, is such a man. As a businessman, Baldwin realized that all engineers need new skills within months of their graduation; as an educator, he imagined an institution through which these skills could be delivered. He knew, further, that companies would pay to have their employees kept abreast of current engineering theories and applications—it was to their advantage, after all, to have first-rate engineers. If these engineers were to gather advanced degrees in the process, the company would be willing to pay the costs. At the same time, Baldwin saw that such education could be provided in a relatively low-cost manner. There was no need, he realized, to create new courses; all that was needed was a new way to deliver existing courses to a new audience. This was Baldwin's vision; NTU is the concrete realization of that vision.

NTU quickly became established as a primary source of graduate engineering education at their work sites. NTU offers working professionals the opportunity to pick and choose from courses originating at any one of its 47 member colleges and universities. Together, NTU members have given courses to many thousands of students at many of the country's biggest companies, including AT&T, Honeywell, Eastman Kodak, and Hewlett-Packard.

Unlike the other consortia in this chapter, NTU is an accredited, degree-granting institution. It offers 16 master's degrees, mostly in a variety of engineering specialties. Courses are delivered by satellite; true to its engineering orientation, NTU was the first major distance-learning institution to switch over to digital transmission—since only digital technology allows NTU to afford to broadcast 24 hours a day, seven days a week, on 14 channels. (All participating universities had to make the technological transition along with NTU, since the schools within the consortium operate the uplinks.) The technological switch has meant a bonanza for students—NTU currently offers the largest array of distance-learning courses of any degree-granting organization in the country.

The relationship between NTU and its partner colleges has been knowingly honed over time. Faculty committees for each program allow professors from each organization to review all new courses and evaluate current offerings. Nearly two-thirds of NTU member institutions accept a single standard tuition rate. The others demand a higher per-credit rate. A split of fees between NTU and its sponsoring institutions keeps the universities committed to the program. At the same time, NTU takes all of the administration off the shoulders of the university. Such areas as registration, transcripts, grades, texts, and exams are all handled efficiently by NTU. Library resources come from any of the colleges, corporations, public libraries, and electronic libraries.

The whole operation benefits everyone. Corporations, for their part, are grateful that their workers can earn degrees without leaving their jobs or costing the corporations travel expenses. The "sponsoring organizations" (that is, corporations who pay for their workers to take courses) offer facilities for classrooms and laboratories, as well as computers and software to allow each course to take full advantage of the technology.

Students wanting to register for an NTU program must show what NTU deems an "appropriate" degree from an accredited baccalaureate-granting institution, and an undergraduate grade point average (GPA) of 2.5. Those who have degrees not related to engineering must demonstrate that they are capable of the work involved, documenting any past experiences or courses. It is also possible to audit courses, but auditing students may not engage the faculty in conversation, take examinations, have work evaluated, or receive a grade for the course. As soon as a student registers, he or she is given an advisor who works with that student throughout the program.

A group of site coordinators proctor the courses, assuring the universities that the corporate connection works smoothly (and also assuring that no one attends the course without paying). An annual conference for Site Coordinators assures basic understanding of the rules and regulations of NTU and helps give NTU a stronger sense of what's working and what isn't.

In 1997, the operations of NTU extended to the Pacific Rim with three degrees and three noncredit courses. The plan is to spread NTU further internationally as each expansion is analyzed and optimized.

The advantages of distance learning NTU-style are great. There's the great variety of courses and degree programs and the weighty reputations of many of the participating universities. The convenience factor for both student and company is considerable. What's more, many courses are taped at work so that the student can watch them at home, accompanied at each side's convenience by online interaction with the faculty. NTU has emerged as a prestigious organization giving degrees that represent rigorous education. This model is one that other organizations may well emulate in the future.

Still, there are some downsides. First, don't bother with NTU if you're not an engineer. Second, even fact-oriented, no-nonsense engineers may well deserve a bit more sophisticated teaching presentations than is the usual manner for NTU courses. Most are strictly lecture, with a professor writing on a chalkboard, barely conversing with any students. No one seems to care about production values as long as the figures of the formulae are clear. This is economical, to be sure, and maybe it works for the audience in question. But there may be something missing when a teacher, in whatever subject area, using a visual medium, neglects to think about or attempt to create a visually sensitive curriculum.

Or maybe this is just how engineers like it. To be sure, NTU has grown to be a huge force by looking at the customer corporations and fulfilling their needs. Its research arm constantly looks at new technologies and new databases. If you are an engineer seeking distance learning, you may not need to look further.

Western Governors University

The distance-learning world is sitting on the edge of its collective seat as the governors of 14 states and one territory (Guam) work to forge a mighty new virtual educational entity, the Western Governors University (WGU). While the motivation was initially economic, this looks to all observers to be the boldest and most far-reaching experiment in the annals of distance learning. Although no courses have yet been offered, the depth and breadth of the planning effort behind WGU to date (not to mention a decided bent towards overturning many traditional bureaucratic tendencies within academia) warrants inclusion here among the big guys.

The vision of the Western Governors Association (the existing organization behind WGU) is pretty simple: a belief that technology can help the western states deliver quality postsecondary education to residents cost-effectively, via sharing of resources and economies of scale. An important part of this vision is the idea that this education should be based on competency rather than the awarding of credits or the spending of hours in class. That is, students must demonstrate through projects and simulations that they have acquired specific skills and that they can solve problems using their new skills. In the liberal arts, they must demonstrate the ability to make broad generalizations, to think beyond the pages that they read. If this happens in eight weeks or ten weeks or twenty weeks, the course is completed. It is no longer necessary for a college to be tied to a 15-week semester, so many hours per week. They are now assuring that their graduates really have command of the material. What a concept.

To turn this vision into reality, needless to say, has required a great deal of compromise and negotiation. Joint actions such as the awarding of credit, the establishment of tuition, the acceptance of joint standards, and the need for each institution to accept teaching from outside its own faculty all require a level of sacrifice and understanding rarely seen in academic circles. Combine the new paradigm presented by distance learning with a move towards competency-based standards and all sorts of existing bureaucratic assumptions and procedures are thrown into a tizzy. The federal government is accustomed to traditional colleges and universities. This distance-learning stuff, with different hours and work at home, does not fit into the programs that they have set up for administering financial aid. The fact that every state and so many Governors are now involved in distance learning puts great pressure on the feds to change their requirements.

The effort of getting a large group of independent institutions from a number of different states to act as one unit has been fraught with academic and bureaucratic difficulties you don't really want to or have to know about—trust us. In the end, however, something pretty interesting has emerged.

First of all, the states have agreed that students will be able to take courses from any of the participating colleges or universities while being able to name the one from which the degree comes, even if it's a different institution. They have also agreed to allow (but not require) schools to make no distinction between in-state and out-of-state students. Each of these agreements at least potentially points to a brave new future for higher education—a future in which time and distance are inconsequential.

For companies hiring students from WGU the switch to competencies rather than credits will bring a better work force, able to accomplish problem solving, reducing the in-house training necessary before a new hire becomes productive. This could be an important trend for all of education. In competency-based learning, what is important is demonstrating what you know—both in the way of skills and knowledge—and how you can use this information to think or to do your job. It's not just about learning facts and spitting them back on a test. The corporate world has recognized this reality long before academics.

WGU is reaching out to other course-producing institutions and consortia, including many mentioned here, as additional providers of good instruction. While their goal is to offer a selection of degrees and courses, the board recognize that not all must be home grown. When they could accept the best of their fellow western states, their minds were open to an acceptance of programs from around the country. At the same time, WGU is not dependent upon one delivery system, but is looking at all available and appropriate technologies.

And this whole process is happening with a very aggressive timeline: Barely two years ago it was just a dream. Within a year from now, we should see the realization of that vision.

Let the Future Begin . . .

There are many more consortia of colleges and universities. There are some very important business ventures such as Westcott Communications and Caliber Learning that are part of both the history and the future of distance learning. As these larger organizations demonstrate, there continues to be great movement in the technologies used for courses. Some are predicting that all will come together (or, to use the buzz word, *converge*) on the Web—when, that is, the "pipes" are large enough to accommodate full video without endless waiting. Meanwhile there is enormous energy in experimentation. Don't expect the dust to settle; simply run alongside and join the fun. Your road to a distance-learning degree is right before you. Enjoy the ride.

Chapter Four

Program Listings

Note: The information in these listings applies only to each school's distance-learning program and not to the school as a whole. The absence of any field of information indicates that either the field is not relevant to that school's program or that the institution could not or did not provide this information.

A*DEC

A*DEC is a consortial organization that does not award degrees directly to students. For a description of A*DEC's offerings and a list of A*DEC member institutions, see chapter 3.

Address

Box 830952
University of Nebraska—Lincoln
Lincoln, NE 68583-0952

Phone:	(402) 472-7000
Fax:	(402) 472-9060
E-mail:	jpoley@unl.edu
URL:	http://www.adec.edu

Contact Person
Janet Poley, A*DEC President

Description

A*DEC is a nonprofit consortium of 50 land-grant colleges and universities that provides and markets high-quality courses, continually staying abreast of the latest in distance-learning technology. A*DEC offers diverse services to members, including current information and immediate resources on topical issues, opportunities for small research grants, and the ability to transfer and trade courses. Its Web page is updated twice daily. A*DEC is characterized by its strong partnerships with a variety of important educational and governmental agencies and institutions.

Admissions Information

Academic Disciplines
Food and agriculture; children, youth, and families; community and economic development, distance education and technology, environment and natural resources, and nutrition and health

Degrees Offered
Master's degree in human resources and family sciences from the University of Nebraska at Lincoln and other degrees from participating universities

Admissions Requirements
Determined by individual member institutions

Equipment Requirements
Depends upon the course

Tuition and Other Fees
Depends upon the participating organization

Credits Transferable?
Yes

Overall Program Information

Delivery System
Works with all appropriate technologies, including satellite, videoconference, audioconference, the Internet, and broadcasts

Year Established
1989

Total Number of Courses
Several hundred

Number of Faculty
Several hundred

Student Demographics
Ranges from traditional on-campus students to professionals to the elderly

Dropout Rate
No aggregate information is available

Accreditation
Individual universities and colleges are all regionally accredited.

American College

Address

270 South Bryn Mawr Avenue
Bryn Mawr, PA 19010-2196

Phone: (610) 526-1000
Fax: (610) 526-1310
URL: www.amercoll.edu

Contact Person
G. Steven McMillan, Ph.D., Director, Graduate Academic Affairs
Phone: (610) 526-1368
E-mail: stevem@amercoll.edu

Description

American College offers two master's degree programs that are designed explicitly for financial services professionals. Both programs combine the convenience of distance learning with the indispensable student-faculty interaction that comes with on-campus residency. The curriculum emphasizes problem solving, analytical and communication skills in course work, and an independent research project. Flexible scheduling, with a course load determined by individual preferences, permits students to set their own pace in planning their program. The Master of Science in financial services, offered through the Graduate School of Financial Sciences, prepares its graduates to become advisors with a diverse financial education, who can handle a whole spectrum of sophisticated client financial needs. The Master of Science in management, offered through the Richard D. Irwin Graduate School of Management, focuses on the knowledge needed to enhance the student's understanding of the components of leadership and management.

Admissions Information

Academic Disciplines
Financial science, management

Degrees Offered

Master of Science in financial services, Master of Science in management

Admissions Requirements

An undergraduate degree from an accredited college or university and a transcript from that college

Tuition and Other Fees

Approximately $8,700. Residency is included, but textbooks are extra.

Credits Transferable?

Yes. Up to nine credits may be accepted from another accredited college or university. Graduate-level courses must be similar in content to those of American College, and credit must be earned during the seven years preceding the student's application to this program.

Program Information

Delivery System

Distance-learning courses come with an American College study guide, which supplements the recommended textbooks. These are self-study courses, though occasionally a number of students may form their own study groups. Delivery via the World Wide Web, video, and CD-ROM is not available at this time. Residency courses are given in the traditional classroom setting.

Year Established

1976

Number of Courses

20

Number of Faculty

24

Student Demographics

Students come from all parts of the country, and around the globe. This year's graduating class of 91 people came from 27 states, Puerto Rico, and Chile.

Accreditation
Commission on Higher Education of the Middle States
Association of Colleges and Schools

Class Information

Average Class Size
20 (during residency)

TAs for Large Classes?
No

Length of Session or Semester
There are two one-week residency sessions. Otherwise, the program is flexible according to the student's needs.

Sessions Required for Degree
Thirty-six credits required for graduation, 12 of which are earned during the residency period.

Time Commitment per Course
Very flexible, according to the student's needs.

Participation Expected
See above

Access to Faculty
E-mail, phone, and fax, plus in-person contact during residency.

Grading Procedure
Traditional

Testing Procedure
Two-hour, computer-based, objective exam administered through a nationwide network of test centers

Telling Details

Remote Access to Library
No

Other Library Resources Available or Recommended
No

Arizona State University

Address

Distance Learning Technologies
P.O. Box 89204
Tempe, AZ 85287-2904

Phone: (602) 965-6738
Fax: (602) 965-1371
E-mail: distance@asu.edu
URL: http://www.asu.edu

Description

Arizona State University offers a Master of Science in Engineering degree through an inexpensive video system for residents of nearby areas. Arizona's business and technology courses have been recognized for their quality. A great many technologies are used in the undergraduate programs: CD-ROM, the Internet, cable, public television, satellite, microwave, and videoconferencing. The master's degree program has yet to incorporate these technologies, although it will change from a correspondence degree to a full visual program. At the same time, Arizona also is a member of NTU and offers some of its courses through the NTU graduate program.

Admissions Information

Academic Disciplines
Engineering

Degrees Offered
Master of Science in engineering; major in electrical engineering

Admissions Requirements
Bachelor's degree from an accredited school

47

Equipment Requirements
A receiver dish for the program's Instructional Television Fixed System (ITFS), wiring, stop box

Tuition and Other Fees
$105 per student credit hour (most courses are three credits).

Credits Transferable?
Depends on the other institution

Overall Program Information

Delivery System
Interactive television. Real time is necessary.

Year Established
The original correspondence course was established in 1935, and the use of video began in 1955. The engineering degree was first offered in 1982.

Number of Courses
85

Number of Faculty
85

Student Demographics
Depends upon the program. The average age is 31 with a range between 21 and 51. In the M.S. program, 85 percent of the students are male.

Dropout Rate
Not available

Accreditation
North Central Association of Schools and Colleges

Class Information

Average Class Size
8–10

TAs for Large Classes?
If faculty requests assistance

Length of Session or Semester
15 weeks

Sessions Required for Degree
Distance learning students normally take one course per semester

Time Commitment per Course
Identical to on-campus courses

Participation Expected
Depends upon the individual faculty member. There is a good deal of homework.

Access to Faculty
Accessible by phone or E-mail

Grading Procedure
A–F

Testing Procedure
Tests are administered and proctored from corporations and public sites.

Telling Details

Average Class Load per Instructor
Most faculty teach on site. There are 8–10 additional students who participate from a remote location. The average class load is three courses.

Faculty Compensation
Distance teaching is part of their class load. Other workload issues are presently under discussion.

Remote Access to Library?
Card catalog access and various databases are online. Use of the Interlibrary Loan system is also permitted.

Other Library Resources Available or Recommended
Local libraries

Athabasca University

Address

Center for Innovative Management
301 Gradin Park Plaza
22 Sir Winston Churchill Drive
St. Albert, Alberta, Canada
T8N 1B4

Phone: (800) 561-4650
Fax: (800) 561-4660
E-mail: cimoffice@cs.athabascau.ca
URL: http://www.athabascau.ca

Description

Athabasca's electronic M.B.A. is a modular and very flexible program. It requires interaction among students, and projects may be work-related. Included is an intensive 5-day elective and a comprehensive project that earns the credits equal to one course.

Admissions Information

Academic Disciplines
Business with a focus on agriculture and executive management

Degrees Offered
Advanced Graduate Diploma in Management (AGDM); M.B.A.; M.B.A. in agriculture with the University of Guelph

Admissions Requirements
A baccalaureate degree from an accredited university or college, three years of professional work experience or acceptable professional designation, and five years of management or supervisory experience

Equipment Requirements
IBM-compatible computer with a 486 CPU or better, hard disk with a minimum 500 MB capacity, Windows 3.1 or higher, and a high-quality printer

Tuition and Other Fees
AGDM—$8,500; M.B.A.—$19,500

Credits Transferable?
Depends on the other university

Overall Program Information

Delivery System
The Internet, asynchronous communications

Year Established
1994

Number of Courses
12 (10 required, 2 electives, and one applied project)

Number of Faculty
Fluctuates. There are currently five full-time professors and adjuncts from universities and corporations.

Student Demographics
This is the largest graduate business school program in Canada, with over 330 students in 1996–97 and more than 500 registered for September 1997. The average age of students is 39. Most have full-time jobs and like the applied focus of the program.

Dropout Rate
5 percent

Accreditation
Association of Universities and Colleges (AUCC)

Class Information

Average Class Size
100 students (30 to 40 students per coach)

TAs for Large Classes?
No

Length of Session or Semester
The school operates in phases (see below). Courses run for eight weeks.

Sessions Required for Degree
There are three phases. Phase 1 involves 6 courses, Phase 2 involves four courses, and Phase 3 involves 2 electives and a major project.

Time Commitment per Course
20–25 hours per week

Participation Expected
Group assignments require active participation. Students are judged qualitatively as well as quantitatively. Anywhere from 20 to 60 percent of their final grade depends on their involvement in the class.

Access to Faculty
Lotus Notes® is used throughout the programs. In addition, there is a coaches' corner, where all students see problems and the coaches' responses. Coaches not directly teaching the student will often add their responses.

Grading Procedure
A–D

Testing Procedure
There is a major assignment in each course. At the end of Phase 1, students take a comprehensive exam, which involves a real company with problems. Students learn about the company in advance by researching it on the Internet and contacting the company's management. The "take-home" exam is given late Thursday night and is due the following Monday. It is a group problem, with each student also having a role in the company. There are general questions and some particular to the roles. Phase 2 has a simulation exam.

Telling Details

Average Class Load per Instructor
Adjuncts have 30–40 students.

Faculty Compensation
Not applicable

Remote Access to Library?
The university particpates in the Interlibrary Loan system. Arrangements have been made with all Canadian universities.

Other Library Resources Available or Recommended
Internet access

Auburn University

Address

Graduate Outreach Program
202 Ramsay Hall
Auburn University
Auburn, AL 36849-5336

Phone: (888) 844-5300
Fax: (334) 844-2519
E-mail: durrocl@eng.auburn.edu
URL: http://www.eng.auburn.edu/department/eop/

Description

Auburn sees its graduate-level distance-learning program as combining elements of traditional instruction with untraditional delivery methods. This program is targeted at working professionals, who are expected to keep their full-time jobs while pursuing their course work. Classes are videotaped in on-campus classroom-studios while the class is being held. Distance-learning students receive the tapes (standard VHS format) within two to four days of the class and return them within two weeks.

Admissions Information

Academic Disciplines
Business administration and engineering

Degrees Offered
M.B.A. and a master's degree in engineering

Admissions Requirements
GMAT for business or GRE for engineering, three letters of recommendation, and two official transcripts of all undergraduate and subsequent course work from respective institutions

Equipment Requirements
Television and VCR

Tuition and Other Fees
$221 per quarter hour for the M.B.A., $216 per quarter hour for the engineering degree

Credits Transferable?
Possibly

Overall Program Information

Delivery System
Videotape

Year Established
1984

Number of Courses
Approximately 150 per year

Number of Faculty
93

Student Demographics
Limited to U.S. residents and military with APO or FPO address. The school currently enrolls students in 40 different states.

Accreditation
M.B.A.—American Assembly of Collegiate Schools of Business; *Engineering*—Engineering Accreditation Commission of the Accreditation Board for Engineering and Technology

Class Information

Average Class Size
M.B.A—20 students; Engineering—5 students

TAs for Large Classes?
No

Length of Session or Semester
Quarter system (47 or 48 class days)

Sessions Required for Degree
M.B.A.—58–88 quarter hours. Engineering—45–48 quarter hours

Time Commitment per Course
Varies by course and professor

Access to Faculty
Mail, E-mail, fax, or telephone

Grading Procedure
Varies by course and professor

Testing Procedure
Tests are administered by approved proctors.

Telling Details

Faculty Compensation
Professors are compensated $20 per credit hour per student per quarter.

Remote Access to Library?
Yes

Ball State University

Address

College of Business
2000 University Avenue
Muncie, IN 47306

Phone: (765) 285-1931
Fax: (765) 285-8818
E-mail: bsumba@bsuvc.bsu.edu
URL: http://www.bsu.edu/business

Description

Involved in a number of technologies for many years, Ball State offered one of the early distance learning M.B.A. programs. Designed originally for Indiana students, the program has now expanded into Ohio, Kentucky, and New Jersey. This is a traditional M.B.A. program that is delivered nontraditionally. Normally there are both distance and on-site students in each class. The 50 off-site "campuses" give students the opportunity to know one another, and to stay close to home or to the office. There are no residency requirements.

Admissions Information

Academic Disciplines
Business

Degrees Offered
M.B.A.

Admissions Requirements
Minimum GMAT score of 400, minimum AWA score of 3.0, 2.5 GPA

Equipment Requirements
Over 50 viewing sites, equipped with digital teleresponder

Tuition and Other Fees
$126 per credit hour. There are no out-of-state fees.

Credits Transferable?
Check with advisor

Overall Program Information

Delivery System
Satellite and teleresponder (real time)

Year Established
1983

Number of Courses
Depends upon the student; approximately 36 semester hours, 16 courses

Number of Faculty
30

Student Demographics
The average age is 28. Most students have worked for about five years. A total of 55 percent of the students participate at a distance, while 45 percent participate on campus. About 67 percent of students in the M.B.A. program are male.

Accreditation
American Assembly of Collegiate Schools of Business

Class Information

Average Class Size
30

TAs for Large Classes?
No

Length of Session or Semester
15 weeks

Sessions Required for Degree
Two years and four months or three years and four months

Time Commitment per Course
4 class hours and 20 hours beyond class

Participation Expected
All students must attend live classes at more than 50 reception sites in Indiana, Ohio, Kentucky, or New Jersey.

Access to Faculty
A special teleresponse unit used in cooperation with the local phone company.

Grading Procedure
4-point grading system

Testing Procedure
Midterm and final tests are given at eight regional testing locations

Telling Details

Average Class Load per Instructor
9 credit hours per semester

Faculty Compensation
Distance-learning classes are considered part of the regular class load, but faculty receive a bonus package.

Remote Access to Library?
Each site is within 50 miles of a library. The university makes use of the Interlibrary Loan system. The Ball State card catalog is available online.

Other Library Resources Available or Recommended
State libraries are available to students in Indiana.

Boise State University

Address

IPT Office, ET-338
1910 University Drive
Boise, ID 83725

Phone: (208) 385-4457 or (800) 824-7017
Fax: (208) 385-3467 or (208) 342-7203
E-mail: bsu-ipt@micron.net
URL: http://www.idbsu.edu

Contact Person
Jo Ann Fenner, Associate Program Developer

Description

The Master of Science degree in instructional performance technology is intended to prepare students for and advance students in careers in the areas of instructional design, job performance improvement, human resources, training, and training managment. The IPT program equips students with skills needed to identify, analyze, and solve a variety of human performance problems in settings such as industry, business, the military, education, and private consulting.

Admissions Information

Academic Disciplines
Instructional and performance technology

Degrees Offered
Master's degree in instruction and performance training

Admissions Requirements
An undergraduate degree from an accredited institution, a résumé, a one- to two-page essay describing why the program is a good match for the student, and one of the following: minimum

GPA of 3.0 during the last two years of undergraduate studies or a minimum score of 50 on the Miller Analogy Test (MAT) or a minimum score of 500 on the verbal skills section of the GRE.

Equipment Requirements

IBM-compatible computer with a 486 CPU or faster, 16 MB of RAM, VGA graphics capability or better, at least 150 megabytes of free space available on a hard disk drive, Windows 95 or NT 4.0, 28.8 modem, 3.5" floppy drive, CD-ROM drive, sound board with speakers, and the ability to play video files.

Tuition and Other Fees

$315 per credit hour or $915 per three-credit course. In addition, course materials average $100 per course.

Credits Transferable

9 credits

Program Information

Delivery System

A BBS system that is configured as a computer-conferencing environment. Asynchronous computer conferencing is the primary vehicle for delivering instruction. It is a closed-community in which only students enrolled in the program have access. Instructors facilitate class discussion and monitor participation, student understanding of the material, and assignments. The instructional strategies used with this delivery method have resulled in a supportive and cooperative learning environment.

Year Established

1989

Total Number of Courses

25 possible course selections with 6 different courses offered every fall, spring, and summer semester.

Number of Faculty

9

Student Demographics
The average number of years students have spent in their profession is 16. The average age is 44. Students have enrolled from every state in the United States and every province in Canada. Most job titles include training manager, performance improvement specialist, re-engineering designer, instructional designer, and multimedia designer.

Dropout Rate
Thirty percent drop out during the first semester. Ten percent drop out during the second semester. Another 10 percent drop out during the third semester, and no students drop out after that point.

Accreditation
Northwest Association of Schools and Colleges

Class Information

Average Class Size
17

TAs for Large Classes?
Class size never exceeds 20.

Length of Session or Semester
16 weeks in fall and spring; 10 weeks in summer.

Sessions Required for Degree
36 credit hours

Time Commitment per Course
12–16 hours per week

Participation Expected
It is essential that the student participates in the online discussion and assess the course progress at least three times per week.

Access to Faculty
E-mail, fax, phone, online, and mail.

Grading Procedure
A–F

Testing Procedure
All tests are administered online. The culminating activity for the program is a comprehensive oral exam conducted over the phone. An examining committee participates using a speaker system at the university.

Telling Details

Average Class Load per Instructor
One distance-course and one on-campus course per semester.

Faculty Compensation
Faculty receive 1 1/2 credits towards their class load for distance learning.

Remote Access to Library?
Access is granted to the local library, the BSU library, and the Internet.

Other Library Resources Available or Recommended
World Wide Web and the student's local library

Boston University

Address

Manufacturing Engineering Program
15 St. Mary Street
Boston, MA 02215

Phone:	(617) 353-2842
Fax:	(617) 353-5548
E-mail:	manufacturing@bu.edu
URL:	http://www.bu.edu

Contact Person
Jennifer Pilton

Description

This engineering program was one of the first to use videoconferencing as the delivery system. Students from the campus are joined with students from various corporations (at each corporate site) to study together in real time with a faculty member. As much as possible, these students are considered part of the campus community, possessing the rights and privileges of traditional students. In many cases, the program is paid for by the corporate host rather than the students themselves. Students can take up to three courses without credit.

Admissions Information

Academic Disciplines
Engineering

Degrees Offered
M.S. in manufacturing engineering

Admissions Requirements

Undergraduate degree from an accredited university, GRE, and letters of recommendation. Students from countries where English isn't spoken must take the TOEFL.

Equipment Requirements

Room equipped with videoconferencing equipment (PictureTel) and a computer. A modem is optional.

Tuition and Other Fees

$687 per credit (most courses are four credits)

Credits Transferable?

Up to eight by petition (two courses)

Overall Program Information

Delivery System

Videoconferencing (real time)

Year Established

1992

Number of Courses

9

Number of Faculty

7

Student Demographics

Mostly male, midcareer professionals

Dropout Rate

Only those leaving the company or the area drop out.

Accreditation

The undergraduate program is accredited by the New England Association of Schools and Colleges. There is no special accreditation for the graduate program.

Class Information

Average Class Size
20 (some larger)

TAs for Large Classes?
There is one TA for every class taught by videoconferencing. There is also an onsite proctor at each corporate site.

Length of Session or Semester
15 weeks

Sessions Required for Degree
9

Time Commitment per Course
Can't be estimated.

Participation Expected
Faculty encourages strong participation in real-time classes.

Access to Faculty
E-mail and phone. Students are also encouraged to contact their TA.

Grading Procedure
A–F

Testing Procedure
Proctored exams at the corporate or on campus site

Telling Details

Average Class Load per Instructor
One distance-learning class per semester plus an on-campus class

Faculty Compensation
These courses are part of the regular teaching load. Faculty are compensated as though they were teaching on campus.

Remote Access to Library?
Students can access the Mugar Library online, and use any campus facility in person.

Other Library Resources Available or Recommended
All necessary materials are sent to students. Occasionally they may need a library for reference material.

California State University— Dominguez Hills

Address

1000 E. Victoria Street
Carson, CA 90747

Phone: (310) 243-2272
Fax: (310) 243-5127
E-mail: washley@dhvx20.csudh.edu
URL: http://www.csudh.edu/dominguezonline

Description

California State, Dominguez Hills is one of 22 California State University campuses. Located in the city of Carson, midway between the Los Angeles harbor and Los Angeles City Hall, Dominguez Hills began to develop a distance -learning program in 1989. Under the direction of the dean of extended education, the university uses many different modalities for delivering courses to students at a distance, including cable television, digital television, UHF, satellite, videoconferencing and the Internet. In 1996–97, 3,799 students enrolled in 63 distance-learning courses pursuing degrees in management, behavioral science, quality assurance, nursing, and interdisciplinary studies. In addition, the university has a 23-year-old correspondence program offering distance-learning students a master's degree in humanities.

Admissions Information

Academic Disciplines
Management, behavioral science, interdisciplinary studies, quality assurance, education, and humanities.

Degrees Offered
M.B.A., M.A. in behavioral science and negotiation and conflict management, M.S. in quality assurance, M.A. in humanities

Admissions Requirements

M.B.A.—B.S. in Business or nine core courses, GMAT or graduate degree. M.A.—B.A. or B.S. with 3.0 GPA or better in last 60 units. M.S.—B.S. degree in a technical field (or permission from department chair) with 2.5 GPA or better in last 60 units. M.A. in humanities—Undergraduate degree from an accredited program, with 3.0 GPA or better.

Equipment Requirements

M.B.A.—Computer, an account with an Internet service provider (Using Netscape or MS Explorer and a 14.4 modem or faster), television with cable or digital television service or satellite downlink depending on geographical location of student, and telephone. M.A.—Computer, an account with an Internet service provider (Using Netscape or MS Explorer and a 14.4 modem or faster), television with cable or digital television service or CSUSAT downlink depending on geographical location of student and telephone. M.S.—Computer, an account with an Internet service provider (Using Netscape or MS Explorer and a 14.4 modem or faster). M.A. in humanities—Computer with modem (course can also be taken via mail).

Tuition and Other Fees

M.B.A.—$199 a unit. M.A.—$170 a unit. M.S.—$140 a unit

Credits Transferable?

Yes

Overall Program Information

Delivery System

M.B.A.—CSUSAT Satellite, Digital television, Cable television—all real time. Available throughout California. M.A. in behavioral science—CSUSAT Satellite, Digital television, Cable television. All interaction occurs in real time. Available throughout California. M.S.—Internet. Available worldwide. M.A. in humanities—Internet, audiocassettes, print. Teacher education courses—digital television, UHF television, cable television. Available only in southern California.

Year Established
The Master of Arts in humanities was established in 1974. The other programs were established in 1989.

Number of Courses
63 in 1996–97

Number of Faculty
57 in 1996–97. The humanities program involves 73 instructors.

Student Demographics
3,799 enrollments in 1996–97. No further demographic data is available.

Dropout Rate
Low; specifics are not available

Accreditation
Western Association Of Schools and Colleges

Class Information

Average Class Size
M.B.A.—100–120. M.A. in behavioral science.—90–100. M.S. in humanities—maximum of 22. M.S.—30–40. Teacher Education Courses: 400–500

TAs for Large Classes?
Yes

Length of Session or Semester
M.B.A.—13-week classes. M.A.—10-week classes. M.S.—13-week classes. Teacher Education courses: 15-week classes

Sessions Required for Degree
M.B.A.—10 courses, 30 units. M.A in behavioral science.—8 courses, 30 units. M.A. in humanities—30 semester hours. M.S.—11 courses, 33 units

Time Commitment per Course
This varies with each course and each program but one unit of credit has traditionally been defined as 15 hours of class time. The student is usually expected to spend 3 hours outside of class reading and preparing assignments for every hour spent in class.

Participation Expected
Students in programs with an Internet component (M.B.A., M.A.) are expected to check their E-mail at least once a week. Students enrolled in classes that are televised live (M.B.A., both M.A. programs, Teacher Education) are expected to view the broadcast and participate by calling in on the toll-free line. Students in Internet programs (M.S.) are expected to complete their assignments by the due date and communicate regularly with their instructors.

Access to Faculty
E-mail, phone, and fax

All faculty members are evaluated with student evaluations at the end of the course. These evaluations are forwarded to the department and recorded before they are given to the faculty.

Grading Procedure
Varies with the course, the degree, and the instructor

Testing Procedure
Varies with the course, the degree, and the instructor, but there are provisions for proctors if the instructor requires the students to take a supervised examination.

Telling Details

Average Class Load per Instructor
The load for a full-time instructor each semester is 12 units, but it is possible for an instructor to teach one 3-unit course each semester on overload for additional compensation. It is rare for an instructor to teach more than one distance-learning class in a year.

Faculty Compensation
All faculty are compensated for teaching distance-learning courses. Some receive honorariums for developing course materials in

addition to the compensation they receive for teaching the course. Instructors who teach courses with large enrollments receive extra compensation. Tenure credit depends on the type of course the instructor is teaching and the instructor's relationship to the university. Instructors are recruited from a pool of faculty members who have demonstrated an interest in teaching a distance learning course.

Remote Access to Library?

Students can access the library through the Internet for purposes of research. At this time they cannot check out books or materials electronically.

Other Library Resources Available or Recommended

CSUDH distance-learning students have access to libraries at other CSU campuses

Clarkson College

Address

101 South 42nd Street
Omaha, NE 68131

Phone: (402) 552-3041
Fax: (402) 552-6057
E-mail: admiss@clrkcol.crhsnet.edu
URL: http://www.clarksoncollege.edu

Contact Person
Jeff Beals, Director of Enrollment Management
Phone: (800) 647-5500
E-mail: admiss@clrkcol.crhsnet.edu

Description

Clarkson College is a progressive health-sciences institution located in Omaha, Nebraska. Graduate students may study completely through distance learning anywhere in the United States. The college features a Master of Science degree in health services management. Master of Science in Nursing degrees are offered in nursing administration, nursing education, and family nurse practitioner. A nurse practitioner post-master's certificate is also available.

Admissions Information

Academic Disciplines
Health services management, nursing

Degrees Offered
M.S.

Admissions Requirements
Varies by program

Equipment Requirements
Computer, modem, fax, VCR, tape player, voice mail

Tuition and Other Fees
$314 per credit hour

Credits Transferable?
Yes

Program Information

Delivery System
Several different technologies are used for each class. Students must have access to a computer with a modem, fax, VCR, audio cassette player, and voice mail. Additionally, printed information is sent to the students through the mail.

Year Established
1988

Number of Courses
Approximately 50

Number of Faculty
Nine

Student Demographics
Eighty-six percent of the students are female. Students are based in 34 states.

Accreditation
North Central Association of Colleges and Schools, National League for Nursing

Class Information

Average Class Size
Six

TAs for Large Classes?
No

Length of Session or Semester
Fifteen weeks in spring and fall, 10 weeks in summer

Sessions Required for Degree
Varies

Time Commitment per Course
Varies

Participation Expected
Same as on campus courses

Access to Faculty
E-mail, phone, fax, correspondence

Grading Procedure
Varies by professor

Testing Procedure
Varies by professor

Telling Details

Faculty Compensation
Faculty members are compensated, but no tenure credit is given.

Remote Access to Library
Some access is available.

Other Library Resources Available or Recommended
Yes

Colorado State University

Address

Division of Continuing and Distance Education
Spruce Hall
Fort Collins, CO 80523-1040

Phone: (970) 491-5288
Fax: (970) 491-7885
E-mail: askdcde@lamar.colostate.edu
URL: http://www.colostate.edu/Depts/CE

Contact Person
Debbie Sheaman

Description

Colorado State University Resources in Graduate Education, or
SURGE, has been involved in distance learning since 1967, when
it became the first video-based graduate education program in the
United States. More than 350 students have completed graduate
degrees through the program since its inception, and many hundreds of others have taken graduate-level courses for professional
development through this wide-ranging effort. Regular on-campus graduate courses are videotaped in special classroom studios
and tapes are sent to participating site coordinators for distance
learning students.

Admissions Information

Academic Disciplines
Engineering, computer science, business, mathematics, education,
and statistics

Degrees Offered
Master's degrees are offered in agricultural engineering, business
administration, chemical engineering, civil engineering, computer
science, electrical engineering, engineering management program,

environmental engineering, human resource development, industrial engineering, management, mechanical engineering, statistics, system engineering and optimization. Doctoral degrees are offered in agricultural engineering, chemical engineering, civil engineering, electrical engineering, environmental engineering program, industrial engineering, mechanical engineering, systems engineering and optimization

Admissions Requirements

To earn a degree, SURGE students must be admitted to Colorado State University Graduate School. Courses may be taken without admission but any student contemplating degree completion must speak to a departmental advisor prior to registration.

Equipment Requirements

VCR; in some courses, Internet access

Tuition and Other Fees

$312–$364 per student credit hour

Credits Transferable?

All credits are recorded on a Colorado State University transcript and transfer as Colorado State courses.

Program Information

Delivery System

Video

Year Established

1967

Total Number of Courses

An average of 80 courses per semester

Student Demographics

Students from the United States and Canada, including personnel from U.S. military bases

Accreditation
North Central Association of Colleges and Schools

Class Information

TAs for Large Classes?
No

Length of Session or Semester
10–16 weeks, depending on the course of study

Sessions Required for Degree
27–33 credits (3–6 credits per semester are recommended)

Grading Procedure
Proctored examinations, assignments

Testing Procedure
Tests must usually be proctored.

Telling Details

Faculty Compensation
No

Remote Access to Library
Yes

Other Library Resources Available or Recommended
Varies

Cornell University

Address

Office of Distance Learning
187 Ives Hall, Ithaca, NY 14853

Phone: (607) 255-3228
Fax: (607)255-7774
E-mail: ale1@cornell.edu
URL: http://www.ilr.cornell.edu/distlearn/dl.html

Contact Person
Amelia Ellsworth

Description

For the past six years, faculty located in Ithaca have taught classes interactively at a distance in real time using PictureTel's compressed digital video-teleconferencing (VTC) technology. The Cornell University Office of Distance Learning is assisting in the creation of new credit and degree programs and course offerings available to students studying independently and at other institutions. Graduate-level distance-learning course offerings vary from semester to semester; students are encouraged to contact the Office of Distance Learning for a current list of available classes from each of Cornell's 13 colleges. As of now, the Master of Professional Studies program from the School of Industrial and Labor Relations is Cornell's only full-fledged master's degree available via distance learning. This program is offered via video-conferencing to a New York City–based site.

Admissions Information

Academic Disciplines
Varies each semester; contact the Office of Distance Learning for a current list of offerings.

Degrees Offered
Cornell plans to offer a Masters of Professional Studies (MPS) program in industrial and labor relations centered in New York City.

Admissions Requirements
Contact the College of Industrial and Labor Relations for this information.

Equipment Requirements
Fully interactive synchronous classrooms are available in the New York area.

Tuition and Other Fees
Contact the College of Industrial and Labor Relations

Credits Transferable?
Yes

Program Information

Delivery System
Cornell's New York City facilities offer compressed digital transmission mode into and out of the building for low-cost, medium-bandwidth, point-to-point, and multipoint classes. Satellite and full-motion video transmission will also be available.

Year Established
The program starts in 1998.

Number of Courses
60, from a variety of programs and colleges.

Number of Faculty
60

Dropout Rate
Varies from course to course

Accreditation
Yes

Class Information

Average Class Size
10–20

TAs for Large Classes?
Yes

Length of Session or Semester
Four months

Sessions Required for Degree
One year

Time Commitment per Course
Saturdays

Participation Expected
Classes on Saturdays in New York City

Access to Faculty
The use of two-way video, E-mail, chat, voice, and other asynchronous technologies varies from course to course.

Grading Procedure
Varies from course to course.

Testing Procedure
Varies from course to course.

Telling Details

Average Class Load per Instructor
One distance class

Faculty Compensation
Yes

Remote Access to Library
Varies from course to course, depending on location and need

Other Library Resources Available or Recommended
Online resources are available.

Embry-Riddle Aeronautical University

Address

Department of Independent Studies
Graduate Program
600 S. Clyde Morris Blvd.
Daytona Beach, FL 32114–9970

Phone: (800) 866-6271
Fax: (904) 266-7627
E-mail: galloglj@cts.db.erau.edu
URL: http://www.db.erau.edu/dis/graduate_program.html

Description

Embry-Riddle Aeronautical University's graduate degree programs are designed to provide the skills necessary to solve problems of the aviation-aerospace industry both today and in the future. Industry problems from the real world are incorporated into the course work. Case studies, simulation, and other experential exercises are used throughout the curriculum. The program employs state-of-the-art instructional methods and electronic interaction techniques between students and instructors.

Admissions Information

Academic Disciplines
Aeronautical science

Degrees Offered
M.A.S.

Admissions Requirements
GPA of 2.5 or higher at undergraduate institution. Conditional admission may be available for students with a GPA between 2.0 and 2.5. Full admission granted automatically to anyone with a

master's or doctorate degree from a regionally accredited college or university.

Equipment Requirements
IBM-compatible computer with a 386 CPU or higher and a modem.

Tuition and Other Fees
$280 per credit hour (tuition includes course study guide and videotapes); books usually between $50 and $100 per semester; $30 application fee.

Credits Transferable?
A maximum combined total of 12 semester credit hours of transfer and advanced standing credit may be applied to the graduate degree under certain conditions.

Overall Program Information

Delivery System
Videotape and CompuServe. The university has a private forum on CompuServe to facilitate communications between faculty and students and student to student.

Year Established
The graduate program was established in 1993. The undergraduate program is 20 years old.

Number of Courses
17

Number of Faculty
30+

Student Demographics
The average age in the graduate program is 36. Geographic distribution is worldwide.

Dropout Rate
10 percent

Accreditation
Commission on Colleges of the Southern Association of Colleges and Schools.

Class Information

Average Class Size
20 to 25 maximum

TAs for Large Classes?
No.

Length of Session or Semester
Three 15-week terms per year

Sessions Required for Degree
A total of 36 semester credit hours is required to complete the program. All requirements must be completed within seven years from initial application.

Time Commitment per Course
Varies on the student and the subject. Most students report that they spend at least six hours per week on study.

Participation Expected
Conference rooms are set aside for each course. Students are encouraged but not required to participate. The posting of messages on the bulletin board provides everyone with access to the current topic. E-mail is private. Student input and interaction is encouraged.

Access to Faculty
Phone, fax, E-mail, and personal contact are all encouraged.

Grading Procedure
Students receive a grade report for each exam. No grades are released over the telephone.

Testing Procedure
All courses have midterm and/or final exams. Students are responsible for securing the services of a proctor who can administer the exams.

Telling Details

Average Class Load per Instructor
No more than three per semester

Faculty Compensation
Faculty are compensated by a stipend payment per student. Teaching record counts towards tenure.

Remote Access to Library?
Yes

Other Library Resources Available or Recommended
University provides students with a library guide and access to library support via CompuServe and the Internet.

Empire State College

Address

Center for Distance Learning or Office of Graduate Studies
28 Union Avenue
Saratoga Springs, NY 12866-4390

Phone: (518) 587-2100 X300
Fax: (518) 587-2100
E-mail: cdl@sescva.esc.edu
URL: http://www.esc.edu

Description

Empire State College, part of the State University of New York (SUNY) system, has combined some of the best of teaching and learning to design a set of highly personalized programs. The president, James Hall, has been an active spokesman for changing university structures in the light of technological possibilities. The bachelor's degrees awarded through distance learning are numerous. The master's degrees are more limited in the technologies used, primarily Internet and print materials. All students are required to come to the campus several times a year for a face-to-face experience with their faculty mentors. An M.B.A. program that uses models proven successful is being developed. A source of great pride for Empire State is their online Writing Center, which is heavily used by advanced-degree students. The entire program is competency based and requires the mastery of established outcomes. It gives credit for prior learning and takes advantage of technologies for course delivery.

Admissions Information

Academic Disciplines
Accounting, finance, economics, general business, management, marketing, liberal studies, interdisciplinary studies, science, math, technologies

Degrees Offered
M.A. in business and policy studies, M.A. in labor and policy studies; M.A. in liberal studies, M.A. in social policy

Admissions Requirements
Bachelor's degree from an accredited college and three letters of recommendation

Equipment Requirements
A computer and a modem for Web-based courses

Tuition and Other Fees
$1,298 (in state) and $2,126 (out of state) per term, $300 one-time assessment fee

Credits Transferable?
Cross-registration from college

Overall Program Information

Delivery System
Print, residency for a few days, E-mail, Internet

Year Established
1984

Number of Courses
100–110 (83 electives)

Number of Faculty
100

Student Demographics
Adults who are already involved in their careers and looking to advance. The average age is 41. The ratio of males to females in business courses is 52–48, in the social policy program it is 40–60. Most students come from the "southern tier" of New York State, primarily because of the residency requirement.

Dropout Rate
30 percent

Accreditation
Middle States Association of Colleges and Schools

Class Information

Average Class Size
10–20 (25) in required subjects

TAs for Large Classes?
No

Length of Session or Semester
3–15 week terms, 3–4 day residencies, 16 weeks of independent study

Sessions Required for Degree
6–8 courses per year (64 credits)

Time Commitment per Course
Each 4-credit course requires about 20 hours per week

Participation Expected
Students are expected to have phone contact beyond their Web study for individual tutorials 5–6 times each term

Access to Faculty
Phone, E-mail

Grading Procedure
Students are graded A–D, based on evaluations of their written work and their telephone conversations. The tutor gives an individualized, written narrative evaluation.

Testing Procedure
Some courses give a final exam. It is more routine to have a project, paper, or group presentation during the residency.

Telling Details

Average Class Load per Instructor
65 students per semester for full-time faculty and chairs

Faculty Compensation
This is considered as part of the total class load. Distance teaching, writing, and research has always been valued in tenure decisions.

Remote Access to Library?
SUNY access to their entire system gives broad coverage of full text documents as well as bibliographic information. This includes access to First Search, a browser similar to Gopher in the SUNY library.

Other Library Resources Available or Recommended
An excellent online writing center.

Fielding Institute

Address

2112 Santa Barbara Street
Santa Barbara, CA 93105-3538

Phone: (800) 340-1099
Fax: (805) 637-9793
URL: http://fielding.edu

Contact Person
Sylvia Williams, Director of Admissions
Phone: (800) 340-1099
E-mail: sawilliams@fielding.edu

Description

This highly respected school was founded as a graduate school to cater to the needs of adults seeking advanced degrees in the middle of their careers—people not well served by the campus-oriented restraints of traditional institutions. It programs are based upon "Learning Plans" that are negotiated between the institution and the individual. Each plan includes a personal assessment, a set of goals, a research proposal, and a specific strategy for how the student's goals will be achieved. Students are accepted based on their past experience and proven competencies, demonstrated writing ability, and the depth and rigor of the intended study. Certain programs divide the students into clusters, while others are strictly a one-on-one structure. The Education Leadership program uses a cohort approach, where students collaborate around action research. Fielding is developing additional programs in continuing education that are rigorous yet extremely personal in their implementation.

Admissions Information

Academic Disciplines
Arts, psychology, and education

Degrees Offered
M.A. in organizational design and effectiveness, Ph.D. in human and organization development, Ph.D. in clinical psychology, and Ed.D. in educational leadership and change

Admissions Requirements
Bachelor's degree from an accredited institution and special academic grounding in the field

Equipment Requirements
Internet access

Tuition and Other Fees
Varies by program; psychology and human development each charge $11,650 per year

Credits Transferable?
Negotiable

Overall Program Information

Delivery System
Internet and face-to-face instruction on location

Year Established
1974

Number of Courses
Varies by program

Number of Faculty
75

Student Demographics
Adults in midcareer. The average age is 40.

Dropout Rate
40 percent

Accreditation
Accrediting Commission for Senior Colleges and Universities of the Western Association of Schools and Colleges

Class Information

Average Class Size
Instruction takes place in small clusters or individually.

Length of Session or Semester
Based on contracts.

Sessions Required for Degree
Two- to five-day sessions on-site each semester

Time Commitment per Course
20 hours per week

Participation Expected
The entire program requires intense interaction with faculty.

Access to Faculty
Internet, E-mail, telephone, and face-to-face interaction on-site

Grading Procedure
Based on competency

Testing Procedure
Individually negotiated with faculty

Telling Details

Average Class Load per Instructor
No classes, many advisors

Remote Access to Library?
All students receive training on Fielding's electronic database. Arrangements are also made with local research libraries.

Other Library Resources Available or Recommended
Online resources, many publications

Florida State University

Address

School of Information Studies
Florida State University
Tallahassee, FL 32306-2100

Phone: (850) 644 5775
Fax: (850) 644 9763
E-mail: logan@lis.fsu.edu
URL: http\\www.fsu.edu

Contact Person
Elisabeth Logan
E-mail: logan@lis.fsu.edu

Description

In this master's degree program, taught through interactive television courses, students will gain the basic theoretical foundation,
knowledge, and introductory skills necessary to function effec-
tively in entry-level professional positions in the field of library
and information studies.

Admissions Information

Academic Disciplines
Information studies

Degrees Offered
M.S., Specialist (an advanced master's degree). The M.S. is avail-
able nationwide, but the Specialist degree is available only in
Dade County, Florida.

Admissions Requirements
For the master's degree program: Possession of a baccalaureate
degree from an approved college or university and a GPA of at
least 3.0 on the last two years of the baccalaureate degree (or a 3.0

in a master's degree program from an accredited university) or minimum score of 1,000 on the combined verbal and quantitative portions of the Graduate Record Examination (GRE). Presentation of a minimum TOEFL score of 550 by international students. All students must submit a GRE score regardless of GPA.

Equipment Requirements

Students are required to have a convenient, graphical access to the Internet. Hardware requirements include the following: a CPU running Windows or Mac OS 7.5 or higher, a high resolution color monitor, keyboard, mouse, and a 28.8 bps or higher modem (unless you have direct connectivity to the Internet). A printer is optional: Many students prefer to print course materials and work with them offline. Some courses may require additional hardware such as a CD-ROM player or sound board. Software requirements include a word processing program. Additional required software may be distributed at registration and as required for future courses. Some students will find a spreadsheet and a database program useful. You may need to purchase additional software for courses with specific needs. Internet connectivity will normally be accomplished through an internet service provider or internet access provider: Students should select a provider that offers PPP connectivity, supports telnet, and offers local or 800 dial-up service. Florida State University has established a contract with IBM Global Net to provide discounted service for its students. A disk kit will be provided free to registered students. This kit will include the information you need to begin service.

Note: Students who use America Online, Prodigy, or Compuserve may encounter some compatibility problems with some of the course requirements.

Tuition and Other Fees

Fees are set by the legislature and the board of regents. The fees include tuition and auxiliary costs for distance education delivery, which includes the technology and local personnel costs. Off-campus fees for fall 1997 is $590 per 3-credit course for Florida residents and $1,506 for out-of-state residents.

Credits Transferable?

Transfer of courses not counted toward a previous degree from another regionally accredited graduate school is limited to six semester hours and transfer of courses not counted toward a previous degree within Florida State University is limited to 12 semester hours, except when the departmental course requirement exceeds the 32-hour university-wide minimum requirement. In the latter case, additional transfer credit may be allowed to the extent of the additional required hours. All transfer credit must be recommended by the department, be evaluated as graduate work by the evaluation section of the office of admissions, and have been completed with grades of 3.0 (B) or better.

Overall Program Information

Delivery System
Interactive television. Class members meet to view together. Real time varies, depending on the class.

Year Established
The distance-learning program was established in 1996. The School of Information Studies was established in 1947 as a professional school.

Number of Courses
18

Number of Faculty
14

Accreditation
American Library Association

Class Information

Average Class Size
Varies

Length of Session or Semester
16 weeks

Sessions Required for Degree
36 credits are required for the master's degree

Time Commitment per Course
Varies

Participation Expected
Varies depending on the class.

Access to Faculty
Because classes are taught via interactive television, the professor and students are interacting with each other regardless of where the professor is located. Some faculty have been meeting before or after class to answer students' concerns or questions. Faculty have E-mail and office hours, and they engage in online chats.

Grading Procedure
Varies

Testing Procedure
Varies

Telling Details

Average Class Load per Instructor
The teaching load aimed for is two courses each term.

Faculty Compensation
Considered as a regular teaching load.

Remote Access to Library?
The FSU Card issued to students gives them access to all State University System libraries. Students can access LUIS, the online catalog, in any of the libraries or through the Web. LUIS includes all of the items located in the SUS libraries, including FSU, as well as access to 64 specialized databases through FirstSearch. A staff member at the Goldstein Library at FSU will be available to provide assistance and interlibrary loans for distance education students via phone and E-mail.

George Mason University

Address

4400 University Drive
Fairfax, VA 22030

Phone: (703) 993-1499
Fax: (703) 993-2392
E-mail: tgroves@gmu.edu
URL: http://www.site.gmu.edu

Contact Person
George Umberger, Assistant Dean
Phone: (703) 993-1520

Description

Five institutions—the University of Virginia, Virginia Polytechnic Institute, Virginia Commonwealth University, George Mason University and Old Dominion University—have developed and produced courses that are delivered by satellite. These courses represent a cross-section of engineering subspecialties. While only some of these universities produce course content, all are receive sites. For all, this represents a fiscally and academically important trend towards sharing of information and course offerings. It is a model that deserves to be replicated. George Mason University also has a reputation for research into new technologies and delivery systems.

Admissions Information

Academic Disciplines
Engineering and Information Management

Degrees Offered
M.S. in computer science; Master of Engineering degrees in information systems, operations research and management, software

systems engineering, statistical science, and systems engineering; Ph.D. in information technology and engineering.

Admissions Requirements
A bachelor's degree for the master's program, a master's degree for the doctoral program, a 3.0 to 3.5 GPA (depending on the program). Students from countries where English is not spoken must take the TOEFL.

Equipment Requirements
Satellite downlink and a corporate or university site

Tuition and Other Fees
$179 per credit hour for in-state students; $510 per credit hour for out-of-state students

Credits Transferable
Six

Program Information

Delivery System
Satellite (real time)

Year Established
1983

Number of Courses
19 each semester

Number of Faculty
Everything comes from other schools; George Mason does not produce or uplink course content.

Student Demographics
Most students are from Virginia. They are middle managers, professional, and mostly male.

Dropout Rate
Difficult to determine. Some students at remote sites choose to complete their program on campus.

Accreditation
Southern Association for Colleges and Schools

Class Information

Average Class Size
45–60

TAs for Large Classes?
Yes

Length of Session or Semester
15 weeks

Sessions Required for Degree
30 credits

Time Commitment per Course
9 hours

Participation Expected
Two-way audio requires student participation. Many courses are in lecture format.

Access to Faculty
Telephone, audiobridge, fax, and E-mail

Grading Procedure
A–F

Testing Procedure
Written and oral exams

Telling Details

Remote Access to Library?
Yes

Other Library Resources Available or Recommended
Web sites

George Washington University

Address

ETL Program
2134 G Street NW, Suite B-6
Washington, DC

Phone: (800) 777-6463, (202) 994 1701
Fax: (202) 994-2145
E-mail: www@www.gwu.edu
URL: http://www.gwu.edu

Description

A distinguished university, GWU has been one of the pioneers in using cable television as a vehicle for instruction. The Educational Technology program is both rigorous and enjoyable for students. Jones Education Company, under its College Connection division, broadcasts the program and takes care of such matters as registration, book orders, grades, and transcripts. At the same time, students must be accepted by GWU in order to enroll. Frequent guest lectures and extensive use of resources are part of each course. Cable programs can be taped and viewed at the student's convenience. Recently, GWU has joined with National Technological University (NTU) to deliver an International M.B.A. In this case, the student would receive credit from GWU but graduate from NTU. This is an important innovation, for it brings an international perspective and audience who will see the benefits of other GWU courses.

Admissions Information

Academic Disciplines
Education

Degrees Offered
M.S. in education and human development in technology, M.F. in project management (from the business school), M.S. and Ph.D. in public health and health services

Admissions Requirements
An undergraduate degree from an accredited institution, a 2.75 cumulative average or better, a score above the 50 percent percentile on the GRE or GMAT, and letters of recommendation. Students from countries where English is not spoken must score above 550 on the TOEFL.

Equipment Requirements
Cable television, computer, CD-ROM

Tuition and Other Fees
$725 per course.

Credits Transferable?
Yes, if approved

Overall Program Information

Delivery System
Interactive instructional television (real time), E-mail, videoconferencing (both synchronous and asynchronous), videoconferencing, videotapes, satellite, multimedia, CD-ROM

Year Established
1985

Number of Courses
6 new courses each semester

Number of Faculty
25

Student Demographics
Professional women in midcareer are the heart of most programs. The average age is 35. They tend to have families and jobs while still finding time for a demanding program of studies.

Dropout Rate
Currently five percent. GWU has an aggressive program to to make students feel like they are part of a program and a community. There are assigned mentors who follow up with students when they begin to miss assignments.

Accreditation
North Central Association of Schools and Colleges

Class Information

Average Class Size
Over 100 in the education technology program; 50–60 in the others.

TAs for Large Classes?
An adjunct faculty member is assigned to the course for every 20 students.

Length of Session or Semester
Fifteen weeks in the older programs. GWU is trying to move to a more flexible arrangement.

Sessions Required for Degree
Thirty-six hours (12 hours of electives in specialization). Some programs vary from this schedule.

Time Commitment per Course
5–10 hours per course per week

Participation Expected
Participation is essential and required, regardless of the technological delivery system. The Internet is used heavily for both real time and asynchronous conversations.

Access to Faculty
E-mail

Grading Procedure
A–D, based on participation and project orientation

Testing Procedure
3-hour comprehensive exam proctored locally by computer or on paper

Telling Details

Average Class Load per Instructor
One distance-learning class per semester in addition to classes on campus.

Faculty Compensation
There is recognition of teaching time.

Remote Access to Library?
Access is granted to local library. Limited access is granted to the GWU library and the bibliographic part of the Interlibrary Loan system.

Other Library Resources Available or Recommended
For the new technology courses, there is a Web resource that includes a library of full text documents on a database.

Georgia Institute of Technology

Address

Center for Distance Learning
620 Cherry Street
Room G-6
Atlanta, GA 30332-0240

Phone: (404) 894-3378
Fax: (404) 894-8924
E-mail: brenda.morris@conted.gatech.edu
URL: http//:www.conted.gatech.edu/distance/
cdl-home.html

Description

Georgia Tech's program involves video recording of both presentation and student-instructor interaction during regular, on-campus Georgia Tech graduate classes. The videotapes and supporting materials are sent to off-campus students, who view the tapes at their convenience. Students enrolled in the program communicate with their professor by telephone, fax, and/or E-mail. Students have access to the Georgia Tech electronic library and the computer system via a business or home computer and a modem. Access is also provided over the Internet. Courses are offered during all four academic quarters of the year.

Admissions Information

Academic Disciplines
Electrical engineering, environmental engineering, industrial and systems engineering, health physics, and mechanical engineering

Degrees Offered
Master's degrees

Admissions Requirements
Each college or department sets their own admission requirements. All students must take the GRE.

Equipment Requirements
VCR and television

Tuition and Other Fees
$297 per credit hour

Credits Transferable?
Each college would examine the credits trying to be transferred.

Overall Program Information

Delivery System
Video tapes are delivered via two-day carrier

Year Established
1977

Number of Courses
Varies from quarter to quarter. There will be about 40 offered in fall 1997.

Number of Faculty
Varies from year to year. Some professors teach distance-learning courses every quarter, while some may teach one quarter per year.

Student Demographics
Most students work full-time while they complete the master's degree. Students are from all over the United States and Puerto Rico. Beginning in fall 1997, international students enrolled in the program.

Accreditation
Southern Association of Colleges and Schools

Class Information

Average Class Size
There may be anywhere from 3 to 40 students taking the course through videotape.

TAs for Large Classes?
Depends on the department.

Length of Session or Semester
Georgia Tech is on the quarter system; each quarter last 10 weeks.

Sessions Required for Degree
Depends on the student's course load. Most complete a degree in three or four years.

Time Commitment per Course
Three hours per week for viewing a typical three-hour course, plus the several hours per week required for reading and assignments.

Participation Expected
Depends on the professor.

Grading Procedure
Each professor sets their own course procedures and requirements

Testing Procedure
Distance learning students are required to have an approved proctor. Tests are administered exactly two weeks after campus test. The proctor receives and administers the exam.

Telling Details

Average Class Load per Instructor
Varies. There are usually at least two courses per quarter.

Faculty Compensation
None

Remote Access to Library?
Yes

Other Library Resources Available or Recommended
Distance-learning students have access to computer accounts at
Georgia Tech.

GMI Engineering and Management Institute

Address

Graduate Studies and Extension Services
1700 West Third Ave.
Flint, MI 48504-4898

Phone: (810) 762-7494 or (800) 955-4464, ext. 7494
Fax: (810) 762-9935
E-mail: bbedore@nova.gmi.edu
URL: http://www.gmi.edu/official/acad/grad

Contact Person
Betty Bedore
Phone: (810) 762-7494

Description

Founded in 1919 and formerly known as the General Motors Institute, GMI took its current name in 1982. This well-respected institution has been providing distance education for 15 years and is beginning to become a provider of note. On-campus presentations are shipped out to the learning sites in business and industry by videocassettes along with all of the materials necessary to complete assignments and hold discussions. The school is experimenting with Web-enhanced delivery, and all courses in three degrees can be taken at a distance. GMI is extremely rigorous.

Admissions Information

Academic Disciplines
Management and engineering

Degrees Offered
M.S. in manufacturing management, engineering, and manufacturing engineering (there are two specialties in engineering)

Admissions Requirements
An undergraduate degree from a regionally accredited college for management or from an ABET-accredited engineering program, a math or science background, GMAT or GRE, and two recommendations. Students from countries where English is not spoken must take the TOEFL.

Equipment Requirements
VCR, computer, and modem

Tuition and Other Fees
$ 1,182 per course

Credits Transferable
Yes—up to three courses

Program Information

Delivery System
Videotape

Year Established
Manufacturing Management, 1982; Engineering, 1990

Number of Courses
There are 18 courses, but only three can be taken at a distance.

Number of Faculty
43

Student Demographics
Professionals in engineering and manufacturing

Dropout Rate
40 percent

Accreditation
North Central Association of Colleges and Schools

Class Information

Average Class Size
180

TAs for Large Classes?
No

Length of Session or Semester
12 weeks

Sessions Required for Degree
4 terms per year; three years for management program

Time Commitment per Course
6–10 hours per course

Participation Expected
High—Students must participate at the corporate site and with the professor by telephone.

Access to Faculty
Phone-in calling hours, fax, and E-mail

Grading Procedure
Students are graded on individual performance by the professor of the course.

Testing Procedure
Evaluation of individual performance is on the basis of work submitted.

Telling Details

Average Class Load per Instructor
1 course

Faculty Compensation
Most faculty receive enhanced pay, depending on enrollment.

Remote Access to Library?
Rarely needed, but assistance from the GMI Library is available electronically.

Other Library Resources Available or Recommended
World Wide Web resources

Goddard College

Address

Plainfield, VT 05667

Phone: (802) 454-8311
Fax: (802) 454-1029
E-mail: admissions@earth.goddard.edu
URL: http://www.goddard.edu

Contact Person
Wayne R. Wood, Director of Admissions and Financial Aid

Description

Goddard College's version of distance learning involves what it calls "low-residency, off-campus" education, at both the undergraduate and graduate levels. Distance learning Goddard-style is highly individualized and highly independent, encouraging students to use the innumerable learning resources away from its rural Vermont campus in carrying out its educational programs. The format is aimed at meeting the needs of working adults and those whose family responsibilities or other circumstances make it impossible for them to be residential students. A demonstrated ability to learn independently is a must for Goddard students. Students develop a study plan during their week-long residency; this study plan works like a private syllabus that the student follows independently throughout the semester. The student's educational program at Goddard is not "delivered" by the faculty to the student as much as it is found by the student through outside resources, with close faculty assistance and interaction.

Admissions Information

Academic Disciplines
Business, organization, and community development; history and social inquiry; visual and performing arts; cultural anthropology and multicultural studies; natural and physical sciences; ecologi-

cal studies; media and communication; writing and literature; education and teaching; psychology and counseling; feminist studies; health arts; nature, culture, and healing; social ecology.

Degrees Offered
M.A. in individualized study, education, psychology and counseling, and social ecology. M.F.A. in creative writing, interdisciplinary arts.

Admissions Requirements
The major part of the application is a personal statement in which students write about their educational goals and their readiness and ability to do independent, off-campus study, relating their goals. Transcripts of all previous academic work are required; a bachelor's degree and preliminary study plan are required for all graduate-level work.

Equipment Requirements
None in particular, but Goddard's overall aim is to make use of all relevant new technologies to enhance its off-campus programs.

Tuition and Other Fees
Varies by program; the average is $4,800 per semester.

Credits Transferable?
Yes

Program Information

Delivery System
The study plan, which lays out the work for the course, is developed during the one-week residency at the start of the semester. After that, students and faculty communicate largely through standard mail.

Year Established
1963

Number of Courses
Not applicable—Goddard courses are individual, semester-long study plans rather than traditional courses.

Number of Faculty
60

Student Demographics
Students enroll from 35 states. The average age 30–40.

Dropout Rate
15 percent.

Accreditation
New England Association of Schools and Colleges

Class Information

Length of Session or Semester
Two semesters per academic year

Sessions Required for Degree
Varies by degree

Time Commitment per Course
26 hours a week of study per semester

Participation Expected
There is a required weeklong residency at the beginning of each semester. There must also be a regular (once every three weeks), substantive written exchange between the student and the faculty advisor.

Access to Faculty
Standard mail, E-mail, telephone, Internet chat groups

Grading Procedure
Joint evaluation of student's learning is an ongoing function, culminating in the full descriptive reports students and their advisors write at the end of the semester.

Grading Procedure
None

Telling Details

Faculty Compensation
Yes

Remote Access to Library
No

Other Library Resources Available or Recommended
Distance learning students make extensive use of educational resources in their local area.

Graduate School of America

Address

330 2nd Avenue, Suite 550
Minneapolis, MN 55401

Phone: (800) 987-1133 or (612) 339-8650
Fax: (612) 339-8022
E-mail: admissions@tgsa.edu
URL: http://www.tgsa.edu

Contact Person
Don Smithmier
Phone: (612) 337-5702

Description

This school was designed for people who are interested in graduate programs in education, management, and human services. The classes are primarily online, with some cluster meetings in such major cities as Indianapolis, Detroit, Atlanta, and Washington, DC. There are two models: Online and individual tutorial. It is possible to mix the models and tailor the program to individual needs, although the Ph.D. program requires some one-on-one tutorial.

Admissions Information

Academic Disciplines
Education, business, and human resources.

Degrees Offered
M.S. in education (concentrations in distance education, instructional design, adult learning). There are master's and doctoral programs in education, management, and human resources.

Admissions Requirements
A bachelor's or master's degree from accredited institution and a GPA of at least 2.7 on a 4.0 scale (3.0 for doctoral program). Students from countries where English isn't spoken must score at least 550 on the TOEFL before admission to the for the bachelor's degree program and at least 600 for the master's program.

Equipment Requirements
Computer with a 28.8 modem

Tuition and Other Fees
Required for M.S.: $795 per online course, $375 graduation fee, and $35 application fee. Optional: $295 focused seminar, $595 extended seminar, and $250 independent study course. The Ph.D. program is continuous: The quarterly cost is $2,445 and there is a $675 graduation fee. Extended seminars are required in doctoral program.

Credits Transferable?
Yes

Overall Program Information

Delivery System
All asynchronous conversations and lessons are held on the World Wide Web.

Year Established
1993

Number of Courses
48 credits (12 courses) for master's degree, and 120 quarter credits (includes 16 quarter credits for dissertation) for the Ph.D.

Number of Faculty
30

Student Demographics
Depends upon the discipline. The overall age range is 25–77, and the average age is 44. These are midcareer professionals. There is

a 50–50 male-female ratio. Thirty percent of the students are minorities.

Dropout Rate
30 percent

Accreditation
The program is a candidate for accreditation by the North Central Association of Schools and Colleges. The final vote on accreditation will take place in November 1997.

Class Information

Average Class Size
15

TAs for Large Classes?
Classes are limited to 15. No TAs are necessary.

Length of Session or Semester
12 weeks (8 learning modules)

Sessions Required for Degree
12 courses

Time Commitment per Course
10–15 hours per week

Participation Expected
Each faculty member establishes a minimum discussion requirement for interaction with the professor and with classmates.

Access to Faculty
E-mail

Grading Procedure
Pass/fail/incomplete, unless a letter grade is required by the student's employer.

Testing Procedure
There are no tests.

Telling Details

Average Class Load per Instructor
2 per quarter

Faculty Compensation
All faculty are distance-learning teachers

Remote Access to Library?
Uses University of Alabama in Huntsville Library System (known as the Cybrary)

Other Library Resources Available or Recommended
Many databases and online course files

Indiana University

Address

Office of Distance Learning
School of Continuing Studies
620 Union Drive, Suite 129
Indianapolis, IN 46202-5167

Phone: (317) 274-3449
Fax: (317) 278-0895
E-mail: scs@indiana.edu
URL: http://www.indiana.edu/~iudisted/

Contact
Office of Distance Learning
Phone: (317) 274-3449
E-mail: scs@indiana.edu

Description

More than 70 Indiana University graduate courses are available to students at a distance. The courses are offered primarily to students in Indiana through a variety of delivery systems that include interactive video, the Internet, and independent study by correspondence. IU has eight campuses around the state, all of which are involved in distance learning. Students seeking graduate degrees should obtain approval for specific distance-learning courses from the dean of the school or division from which they expect to graduate and follow normal registration procedures. Students interested in individual courses must select an Indiana University campus to serve as their home campus, and should contact the campus coordinator of the regional campus chosen for more information. Because of the relative decentralization of IU's distance learning offerings, the information provided below tends to be sketchy and generic. The Web site is thorough and up-to-date, so it's a good additional place to check for more details.

Admissions Information

Academic Disciplines
Business; distance learning; education; health, physical education, and recreation; library and information science; nursing; and philosophy

Degrees Offered
Master of Science in education (language and literacy education), nursing, therapeutic recreation, and adult education

Admissions Requirements
Varies by program

Equipment Requirements
Varies by program

Tuition and Other Fees
$147 per credit hour

Credits Transferable?
Varies by program

Program Information

Delivery System
Interactive video (real time), the Internet, independent study by correspondence

Year Established
Varies for each discipline

Number of Courses
73

Number of Faculty
75

Accreditation
North Central Association of Colleges and Secondary Schools

Class Information

Average Class Size
20

TAs for Large Classes?
Yes

Length of Session or Semester
Fall and spring semesters—16 weeks. First summer session—5 weeks. Second summer session—8 weeks.

Sessions Required for Degree
Varies

Time Commitment per Course
Varies

Participation Expected
Varies

Access to Faculty
Not available

Grading Procedure
Varies

Testing Procedure
Varies

Telling Details

Average Class Load per Instructor
Not available

Faculty Compensation
Varies from department to department

Remote Access to Library
Yes

Other Library Resources Available or Recommended
Internet resources as appropriate

International School of Management—ISIM University

Address

501 Cherry Street, Room 350
Denver, CO 80222

Phone: (800) 441-4746 or (303) 333-4224
Fax: (303) 336-1144
E-mail: admin@isim.com
URL: http://www.isimu.edu

Contact Person
Tim Adams
Phone: (303) 333-4223

Description

ISIM received the top Internet award from the United States Distance Learning Association in 1996 for the quality of its online master's degree programs. ISIM was cited in particular for the excellence of its supporting materials, the comprehensiveness of the curriculum, and the bibliographic work surrounding each course. All of the materials are online and in the large notebook that accompanies each course. While there were no graphics accompanying the text in 1996, they have since been added.

Admissions Information

Academic Disciplines
Business and information management

Degrees Offered
M.S. in information management, M.B.A., and a M.B.A. in health care

Admissions Requirements
A bachelor's degree from an accredited institution, transcript, completed application, and a detailed résumé.

Equipment Requirements
Computer, modem, Web browser

Tuition and Other Fees
$275 per credit hour, $50 application fee

Credits Transferable
No

Program Information

Delivery System
Internet

Year Established
1993 (degree programs)

Number of Courses
45

Number of Faculty
35

Student Demographics
Students are participating from around the world—the United States, Canada, Europe, Africa, and Asia. The ages range from 23 to 57. Three times as many men as women participate.

Dropout Rate
2 percent

Accreditation
Distance Education and Training Council

Class Information

Average Class Size
One faculty for eight students

TAs for Large Classes?
No

Length of Session or Semester
Five terms per year, each lasting eight weeks

Sessions Required for Degree
11 sessions plus a capstone project

Time Commitment per Course
Varies from 60–120 hours per course

Participation Expected
Active participation is expected. There are individual and group projects. Each student must log in and respond to the ongoing discussion.

Access to Faculty
Online

Grading Procedure
A, B, and Unsatisfactory

Testing Procedure
Students are tested online and in libraries, where the tests are proctored.

Telling Details

Average Class Load per Instructor
One or two courses

Faculty Compensation
None

Remote Access to Library?
Use of the Internet

Other Library Resources Available or Recommended
Other materials arrive through the mail.

Jones Education Company

International University College
The College Connection

Address

9697 East Mineral Avenue
P.O. Box 6512
Englewood, CO 80155-6512

Phone: (800) 777-MIND (ext. 3157)
Fax: (303)799-0966
E-mail: access from home page
URL: http://www.iuc.edu

Contact Person
Dr. Pamela Pease, Interim Provost, Vice President, and Dean of
Academic Affairs

Description

Dating back to the founding of Mind Extension University, Jones
Education Company has been delivering graduate-level courses
by cable. Today this operation is known as The College
Connection, and Jones has also added an online degree program
called International University College. Students are supported by
individual advisors, special seminars, and study groups. Jones
officials continue to reevaluate their offerings, most recently moving away from a reliance upon visual images to more text-based
learning via the Internet. Courses originate both from traditional,
existing universities as well as from Jones itself; the company's
administrative structure makes everything run smoothly from
online registration to book procurement and from grading to transcripts (see chapter 3).

Admissions Information

Academic Disciplines
Business and technology

Degrees Offered
M.A. in business communication from International University College, M.S. in educational technology leadership from George Washington University, M.B.A. from the University of Colorado

Admissions Requirements
Master's degree candidates must have earned an undergraduate degree from an accredited university or prior approval from the admissions manager. Students may enroll in a course online while awaiting approval (www.international.edu/register).

Equipment Requirements
Internet access (particularly to the World Wide Web), cable access, and a VCR

Tuition and Other Fees
$700 per three-credit course (master's level), $75 application fee, $30 graduation fee, $25 Listserv fee, $50 fee for incomplete course

Credits Transferable?
Dependent upon institution

Overall Program Information

Delivery System
Depends on program. Most programs feature asynchronous communication.

Year Established
1995

Number of Courses
33

Number of Faculty
2 full-time faculty; between 5 and 15 adjunct faculty

Student Demographics
Most students are over 28 in age.

Dropout Rate
5 percent

Accreditation
Candidate for accreditation from the United States Regional Accreditation Agency, North Central Association of Colleges and Schools (NCA). The college has four years to complete full accreditation. All of the partner colleges and universities have full accreditation.

Class Information

Average Class Size
8–10

TAs for Large Classes?
No

Length of Session or Semester
Accelerated 8-week terms

Sessions Required for Degree
13 courses

Time Commitment per Course
14–19 hours per week, depending on content

Participation Expected
Everyone must contribute to the Web-based forum. There are also E-mail and group meetings. There are minimum guidelines for participation

Access to Faculty
E-mail, group meetings

Grading Procedure
There is a study guide and content experts who work with prescribed guidelines for completion of courses.

Testing Procedure
There is little actual testing. Sometimes midterms are given.

Telling Details

Average Class Load per Instructor
8–10

Faculty Compensation
No

Remote Access to Library?
All textbooks and print resources are supplied by JEC, which also has an arrangement with Denver University for interlibrary loans.

Other Library Resources Available or Recommended
Almost all resources are available online.

Lehigh University

Address

Office of Distance Education
205 Johnson Hall
36 University Drive
Bethlehem, PA 18015

Phone: (610) 758-5794
Fax: (610) 758-6269
E-mail: mak5@lehigh.edu
URL: http://www.lehigh.edu/~indis/indis.html

Description

This 132-year-old institution is at the leading edge of satellite technology, delivering all of its distance-learning courses over the Lehigh Educational Satellite Network (LESN), which features digital transmission. A corporate site requires a Ku-Band downlink and a CLI SpectrumSaver digital receiver. Each classroom needs a video monitor, phone, fax machine, VCR and an interactive computer system. Lehigh provides technical information and assistance for any company interested in receiving these programs.

Admissions Information

Academic Disciplines
Chemistry, chemical engineering, quality engineering, molecular biology, and business administration

Degrees Offered
M.S. and M.B.A.

Admissions Requirements
Bachelor's degree from accredited 4-year college, GMAT for M.B.A.

Equipment Requirements
Ku-band satellite receiver and digital decoder

Tuition and Other Fees
$555 per credit hour

Credits Transferable?
Generally six credits may be transferred.

Overall Program Information

Delivery System
Live, interactive digital satellite transmission.

Year Established
1992

Number of Courses
About 260

Number of Faculty
About 50

Student Demographics
Varied

Dropout Rate
Undetermined to date.

Accreditation
Middle States and American Assembly of Collegiate Schools of Business for M.B.A.

Class Information

Average Class Size
Varied

TAs for Large Classes?
Yes

Length of Session or Semester
42 contact hours in fall and spring, and 36 contact hours in summer

Sessions Required for Degree
Varied

Time Commitment per Course
Varied

Access to Faculty
Course evaluations

Grading Procedure
Same as on campus

Testing Procedure
Examinations must be supervised by an approved proctor.

Telling Details

Average Class Load per Instructor
3–5 per year depending on program

Faculty Compensation
No

Remote Access to Library?
Yes

Other Library Resources Available or Recommended
Students are given access to Lehigh's E-mail and computer system

Louisiana State University

Address

Division of Instructional Support and Development
118 Himes Hall
Baton Rouge, LA 70803

Phone: (504) 388-1135
Fax: (504) 388-5789
E-mail: mabbiat@lsu.edu
URL: http://www.lsu.edu

Contact Person
Michael D. Abbiatti, Director of Distance Education

Description

Administered through a collaboration of the University's Division of Instructional Support and the Division of Continuing Education, the LSU Distance Education program features advanced compressed-video technology. Originally designed to supplement the regular curriculum of existing LSU students—notably those on LSU's smaller campuses in Shreveport, Alexandria, and Eunice—the program aims to offer complete degree programs as it grows. Only enrolled LSU students may pursue a graduate degree, but graduate-level courses are available via distance learning to anyone interested on a course-by-course basis, including older, nontraditional students seeking professional development.

Admissions Information

Academic Disciplines
All

Degrees Offered
None at this time

Admissions Requirements
Same as on campus

Equipment Requirements
All equipment is available on site.

Tuition and Other Fees
Same as on campus

Credits Transferable?
Yes

Program Information

Delivery System
Compressed video, satellite (one-way video, two-way audio), audiographics (two-way interactive computer graphics), Internet

Year Established
1995

Number of Courses
Average of 30 per semester

Number of Faculty
Varies. The number grows each semester.

Student Demographics
So far, the student body is comprised primarily of Louisiana students.

Dropout Rate
Very low

Class Information

Average Class Size
10–12 students per site

TAs for Large Classes?
Yes

Length of Session or Semester
Varies. A semester lasts approximately 16 weeks.

Sessions Required for Degree
Varies by degree

Time Commitment per Course
3 contact hours per week, on the average

Participation Expected
As much as possible

Access to Faculty
E-mail and toll-free telephone

Grading Procedure
Varies by course

Grading Procedure
Varies by course

Accreditation
Southern Association for Colleges and Schools

Telling Details

Average Class Load per Instructor
Varies

Faculty Compensation
Varies, depending on the department

Remote Access to Library
Yes

Other Library Resources Available or Recommended
Varies

Massachusetts Institute of Technology

Address

77 Massachsetts Avenue
Room 9-234
Cambridge, MA 02139

Phone: (617) 253-2836
Fax: (617) 253-8301
E-mail: caes@mit.edu
URL: http://www-caes.mit.edu

Description

One of the world's leading educational institutions, MIT is divided into five schools with 21 academic departments as well as many interdepartmental programs, laboratories, and centers. The Center for Advanced Educational Services offers various undergraduate and graduate programs via distance learning, using different technologies in combination. The first model is called a "Distributed Classroom," in which interactive telecommunications technologies extend a classroom-based course from one group of learners to another. The second model is called "Independent Learning." Students are provided with materials, a course guide and syllabus, and access to a faculty member who provides guidance, answers questions, and evaluates student work. This can take place in person or by using the World Wide Web, E-mail, or videoconferencing. The third category is called "Strategic Partner Relationships," which involves the redistribution of MIT content to universities and organizations around the world.

Admissions Information

Academic Disciplines
Business, engineering, humanities, architecture, and science (in other words, all five schools at MIT are involved with distance learning).

Degrees Offered
Master of Systems Design and Management

Admissions Requirements
Requirements for taking courses for credit differ slightly from those for students auditing the courses. Both are based on college transcripts, and a letter from a principal in the applicant's organization confirming approval and willingness to provide appropriate support. A summary of objectives and experience should accompany the application. Noncredit students are accepted by MIT based upon their academic training and professional experience.

Equipment Requirements
Videoconferencing, video, access to the World Wide Web, and a videotape player

Tuition and Other Fees
$2,000 per noncredit course and $4,600 per credit course. Academic credit from Strategic Partner Relationships is based upon tuition arrangements established with MIT. There is no financial aid for CAES programs.

Credits Transferable?
Credits from other colleges may or may not be accepted, but all other colleges will accept MIT courses.

Overall Program Information

Delivery System
Videoconferencing in real time; both synchronous and asynchronous conversations on the World Wide Web; video, E-mail, fax. The university recognizes the necessity of maintaining student-professor and student-student interaction. Web-based courses

typically include E-mail, mailing lists, digitized video, animation, photos, figures, charts, and search utilities.

Year Established
1995

Number of Courses
Twelve for credit, eight for noncredit in 1996–97; 20 additional courses will be added in 1997–98

Number of Faculty
20 (over 1,100 possible faculty for the future)

Student Demographics
Mostly midcareer professionals. Presently, international students are from Peru, Argentina, and Chile.

Dropout Rate
0 percent

Accreditation
New England Association of Schools and Colleges

Class Information

Average Class Size
10 on campus, 75 international per course. The university also recognizes that many people are monitoring the course. There may be over 100 nonparticipants.

TAs for Large Classes?
Yes

Length of Session or Semester
Traditional 15-week semester

Sessions Required for Degree
Master's degree should be completed within 24 months

Time Commitment per Course

Classes take place for three hours twice per week. For every hour of class there should be at least two hours of study outside of class.

Participation Expected

One-third of the grade depends upon active participation in "threaded discussions" which can take place publicly or privately through E-mail and fax.

Access to Faculty

E-mail

Grading Procedure

A–D

Testing Procedure

There is an appointed proctor at each site. All tests are administered through the proctor.

Telling Details

Average Class Load per Instructor

Each program is considered part of the professor's normal class load. A professor may choose to offer a course taught on campus at a different time on a fee basis.

Faculty Compensation

There are three forms of compensation—flat fee, royalty schedule, revenue split.

Remote Access to Library?

Yes. Online access. There are future plans to hire a dedicated resource person.

Other Library Resources Available or Recommended

All articles necessary for programs are online, linked by hypertext.

Montana State University

Address

Off Campus M.B.A. Program
Billings, MT 59101

Phone: (406) 657-2158
Fax: (406) 657-2289
E-mail: mba_neu@vino.emc.mt.edu
URL: http://www.msubillings.edu

Contact Person
Sharon Signori

Description

Delivered by interactive audio and video, this program was designed for the working person and encompasses all business courses. Students watch lectures and work with real problem solving. Many of the class assignments demand strong computer and mathematics skills. The program aims to give graduating students a sense of preparedness for the challenges of business.

Admissions Information

Academic Disciplines
Business

Degrees Offered
M.B.A.

Admissions Requirements
The student must score a 950 or better in an index where the student's GPA is multiplied by 200 and added to the student's GMAT score. A bachelor's degree and computer experience with spreadsheets and databases are also required.

Equipment Requirements
A room to access the transmission, computer, modem

Tuition and Other Fees
$275 per credit hour

Credits Transferable
9 credits with grades of B or better

Program Information

Delivery System
Interactive audio and video

Year Established
1988

Total Number of Courses
Two core courses for each program part and five electives

Number of Faculty
Entire school of business

Student Demographics
Working professionals. The average age 35, with a rough balance of male and female students.

Accreditation
American Assembly of Collegiate Schools of Business

Class Information

Average Class Size
30–40

TAs for Large Classes?
No

Length of Session or Semester
4 months

Sessions Required for Degree
30 credits (21 core courses, nine electives). The core courses are three credits each, while electives vary in credits.

Time Commitment per Course
20 hours per week on average

Participation Expected
Part of grade

Access to Faculty
E-mail and telephone

Grading Procedure
A–F

Testing Procedure
All testing is onsite.

Telling Details

Average Class Load per Instructor
Varies

Faculty Compensation
Yes, but no credit is granted towards tenure.

Remote Access to Library?
Yes

Other Library Resources Available or Recommended
No

National Technological University

Address

700 Centre Avenue
Fort Collins,CO 80526

Phone: (970) 495-6430
Fax: (970) 498-0601
E-mail: Gerry@mail.ntu.edu
URL: http://www.ntu.edu

Contact Person
Gerry Johnson

Description

NTU offers more than 500 courses in engineering from 47 prestigious universities. Master's degrees come from NTU itself as an accredited institution.There are 13 M.S. degrees. At present, NTU is initiating courses in management and an International M.B.A. degree, as well as its extensive listings in engineering, with a base in companies throughout the United States. A pilot project on home delivery is currently taking place. See chapter 3 for additional information.

Admissions Information

Academic Disciplines
Engineering, business, and technology management

Degrees Offered
M.S. in engineering (13 subsets), M.S. in technology management, M.B.A. in international business

Admissions Requirements
A degree from an accredited institution (GPA 2.9 out of 4.0) and GRE. Students from countries where English isn't spoken must take the TOEFL or arrange for a personal interview.

Equipment Requirements
Satellite downlink, computer, modem

Tuition and Other Fees
The basic rate is $585 per credit hour. There are other assorted fees in addition to the basic rate.

Credits Transferable?
Yes

Overall Program Information

Delivery System
Satellite, computer conferencing via Internet and E-mail

Year Established
1984

Number of Courses
500 annually

Number of Faculty
None from NTU itself; all come from participating universities.

Student Demographics
Midcareer profesionals. Eighty percent are male.

Dropout Rate
Two percent fail. Fifty percent drop out, but most of these students do so because they change jobs or companies and cannot continue the course.

Accreditation
North Central Association of Schools and Colleges

Class Information

Average Class Size
Eleven. Additional students may take the course for no credit.

TAs for Large Classes?
Generally, yes.

Length of Session or Semester
Varies according to the college. Most are on a semester schedule, while a few are on quarters.

Sessions Required for Degree
30–36 credits

Time Commitment per Course
Same as campus courses. Three hours of study are expected for every hour of class

Participation Expected
Little is expected in engineering courses that rely mostly on workplace projects. Management courses require participation (a phone bridge) during the lessons.

Access to Faculty
E-mail

Grading Procedure
A–F

Testing Procedure
All NTU courses originate on an actual college campus, so distance-learning students and on-campus students take the same tests.

Telling Details

Average Class Load per Instructor
Depends on the university

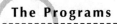

Faculty Compensation
NTU may contribute additional money to pay for faculty.

Remote Access to Library?
Corporate and institutional libraries

Other Library Resources Available or Recommended
Access to online databases

National University

Address

11255 North Torrey Pines Road
La Jolla, CA 92037

Phone: (619) 642-8000
Fax: (619) 642-8709
E-mail: esi@nunic.nu.edu
URL: http://www.nu.edu

Contact Person
Pam Montroy, Admissions Advisor
E-mail: esi@nunic.nu.edu

Description

Founded in 1971, National University is a nonprofit, accredited institution of higher education that specializes in meeting the educational needs of adult learners. NU has 10,000 full-time students. Its academic and administrative center is located in La Jolla, with a main campus in Mission Valley and learning centers located throughout the country. The university's graduate-level offering is known as the "Global M.B.A."—a 12-course program comprised of three modules that enable students from around the world to pursue an M.B.A. while continuing full-time employment or other obligations.

The program's mission is to prepare graduates for upper-level management positions with an emphasis on the global aspects of business and business management. Courses for the Global M.B.A. program are developed through cooperative arrangements with professors from prestigious universities around the United States. All courses strive to reflect the most current theories, issues, and applications in international business management. National University takes full advantage of distance-learning technologies to recruit highly qualified guest faculty members from other notable U.S. institutions of higher education.

The Global M.B.A. combines CD-ROMs, the Internet, and teleconferencing to create a dynamic learning environment for students, including the opportunity for real-time interaction. The program encourages the exchange of information between cultures as students throughout the world collaborate on case studies and use interactive communication tools to discuss relevant issues affecting business in their own countries. Because the program is relatively new, however, the program's demographic makeup has yet to be assessed.

Admissions Information

Class Information
Business administration

Degrees Offered
M.B.A.

Admissions Requirements
A bachelor's degree from an accredited institution with no less than a 2.5 GPA. Applicants with a GPA between 2.0 and 2.5 may be admitted on a provisional status. International students must obtain a minimum TOEFL score of 550 to demonstrate proof of English-language proficiency. Applications for admission are accepted continuously throughout the year.

Equipment Requirements
Computer (PC or Macintosh) with a high-speed link to the Internet. Computer should have a minimum of a 100-MHz CPU, 16 MB of RAM, 1GB hard drive, 4X CD-ROM drive, 14-inch high-resolution color monitor, Sound Blaster audio card (if PC), and Ethernet card (if PC).

Tuition and Other Fees
$200 per quarter-unit (tuition may vary depending upon the country in which the student resides and the arrangement with the host institution), application fee of US$60 or US$100 for international students, graduation fee of $100

Credits Transferable?
Students may transfer up to 15 quarter units of graduate-level course work as reviewed on a case-by-case basis

Program Information

Delivery System
CD-ROMs, World Wide Web, the Internet, video, teleconferencing

Year Established
1996

Number of Courses
12

Number of Faculty
10

Accreditation
Western Association of Schools and Colleges

Class Information

Average Class Size
15

TAs for Large Classes?
No

Access to Faculty
E-mail, telephone, mail. National also has a special software package that can be downloaded from the Internet that acts as an Intranet. Students, faculty, and staff use this software to E-mail, conference, or engage in chat sessions.

Length of Session or Semester
One month is recommended, but the program can take up to four months.

Sessions Required for Degree
12

Time Commitment per Course
60–70 hours

Participation Expected
Students are encouraged to participate through E-mail and online conferences, as well as with other students in class

Grading Procedure
Case studies and final exams determined by professor

Testing Procedure
Submission of case studies to professor for grading and proctored final exams graded by the instructor

Telling Details

Average Class Load per Instructor
Not available

Faculty Compensation
Faculty is compensated the same as professors who are not involved in distance learning

Remote Access to Library
A number of electronic resources are linked through the library's Web pages, including two powerful full-text databases named Info ASAP and Stat USA. Students can also access a complete listing of the library's book collection. Residents of the United States can make Interlibrary Loan requests through their local libraries.

Other Library Resources Available or Recommended
Also available are online references applicable to each course

New Jersey Institute of Technology

Address

Division of Continuing Professional Education
323 Martin Luther King Blvd.
Newark, NJ 07102-1948

Phone: (800) 624-9850 or (973) 596-3640
Fax: (973) 596-3203 or (973) 596-3288
E-mail: cpe@njit.edu or dl@njit.edu
URL: http://www.njit.edu/cpe or http://www.njit.edu/dl

Contact Person
Richard L. Schaatzberg, Director, Development and Marketing
Phone: (973) 596-3641
E-mail: schatzberg@admin.njit.edu

Description

NJIT has been involved in academic computing for almost 20 years. It was one of the first institutions to begin teaching courses through the computer. Now the program is far-reaching with large numbers of classes and courses, including degree and certificate programs at all levels. Although residents of New Jersey constitute a large part of their student body, their doors are open to all who qualify. They work with both interactive television and computers, maintaining frequent contact with the students.

Admissions Information

Academic Disciplines
Computer science, information systems, history, literature, philosophy, mathematics, management, marketing, finance, economics, electrical engineering, engineering management, English, industrial engineering, management of information systems, and physics

153

Degrees Offered
M.S. in information systems, M.S. in engineering management, and several bachelor's and certificate programs

Admissions Requirements
Transcript of an undergraduate degree from an accredited college, a 2.8 GPA from an undergraduate institution that meets NJIT's standards, and GRE or GMAT

Equipment Requirements
Access to a VCR, IBM-compatible computer with a 486 CPU or faster, Windows 95, 16MB of RAM, hard disk with at least 500 MB capacity, and a 14.4 modem

Tuition and Other Fees
Courses are three credits each. $346 per credit for in-state students, $479 per credit for out-of-state) students, $34 per semester non-matriculated application fee, $150 tape leasing fee (per course)

Credits Transferable?
Yes; graduate students are limited to nine transfer credits.

Overall Program Information

Delivery System
Video "tele-lectures" that can be completed from home or office using a VCR and electronic communications with students and faculty through E-mail, Internet, phone, or fax. Interactive television courses in real time with two-way audio and two-way video.

Year Established
1978

Number of Courses
120 (all distance learning programs)

Number of Faculty
80

Student Demographics
Men and women between the ages of 25 and 55. They are generally highly motivated and organized and have effective time management skills.

Dropout Rate
Less than 20 percent

Accreditation
Middle States Association of Schools and Colleges; American Assembly of Collegiate Schools of Business

Class Information

Average Class Size
20

TAs for Large Classes?
Yes

Length of Session or Semester
16 weeks

Sessions Required for Degree
6–9 hours per week (including telelectures and assignments) for each course

Time Commitment per Course
6–9 hours per week, including telelectures and assignments for each course

Participation Expected
Students are asked to communicate with their faculty mentors and classmates at least twice a week by E-mail, Internet, phone, or fax.

Access to Faculty
E-mail and phone

Grading Procedure
Traditional 4.0 scale

Testing Procedure
If students are within 60 miles of campus, they are asked to come to campus for examinations. If not, they nominate a proctor who receives exams from the faculty mentor and administers the exam.

Telling Details

Average Class Load per Instructor
4 courses (12 credits)

Faculty Compensation
Yes

Remote Access to Library?
Yes

Other Library Resources Available or Recommended
Yes

New York Institute of Technology

Address

Online Campus
New York Institute of Technology
P.O. Box 9029
Central Islip, NY 11722-9029

Phone: (800) 222-NYIT
Fax: (516) 348-1107
E-mail: pfenn@acl.nyit.edu
URL: http://www.nyit.edu/olc

Contact Person
Pat Fenn

Stanley Silverman
Phone: (800) 462-9041

Professor William Lawrence (M.B.A. program)
Phone: (212) 621-1595

Description

Don't be put off by the post office box number. There are three physical campuses for NYIT in Old Westbury, Manhattan, and Islip. In these facilities, there is a great deal of experimentation and research surrounding various delivery systems. Each is equipped with two-way teleconferencing, compressed video, and computer conferencing. They are constantly booked by an ever more sophisticated and committed faculty. Sites in Korea, Taiwan, and Chile are used in a research projects. The relatively new online campus is growing quickly as faculty learn to adapt their courses to an online format. The use of fiberoptic modes and ISDN lines between the campuses and other institutions allows NYIT to service many teachers and schools throughout the state as well as offer both undergraduate and graduate programs to anyone in the world.

Admissions Information

Academic Disciplines
Business and behavioral sciences (sociology, psychology, criminology, and community mental health) on the baccalaureate level. A fiberoptic network concentrates on telecommunications and hospitality industries.

Degrees Offered
M.S. in instructional technology (four courses now, growing to a whole program), M.B.A.

Admissions Requirements
Sucessful completion of an undergraduate degree from an accredited institution and GMAT. Students from countries where English isn't spoken must take the TOEFL.

Equipment Requirements
Computer, 28.8 modem, access to graphical interface for Internet

Tuition and Other Fees
$390 per credit (most courses are four credits)
$50 application fee

Credits Transferable?
Subject to evaluation. World Education Services evaluates credits for all foreign students

Overall Program Information

Delivery System
Fiberoptics, compressed video, and computer-based online courses

Year Established
1987

Total Number of Courses
10 for graduate students and 100 for undergraduate students

Number of Faculty
75 (includes those who teach undergraduates)

Student Demographics
Adult students over 22.

Dropout Rate
Characterized by the school as low.

Accreditation
Middle States Association of Colleges and Schools

Class Information

Average Class Size
A class will run even if there is only one student. The upper limit is 25.

TAs for Large Classes?
Unnecessary

Length of Session or Semester
15 weeks (three semesters per year)

Sessions Required for Degree
36–42 credits

Time Commitment per Course
Each student must sign in four times per week. This requires many hours of participation.

Participation Expected
Very high degree of interactive participation in project groups and with faculty.

Access to Faculty
E-mail

Grading Procedure
A–F

Testing Procedure
At the discretion of the instructor, there are proctored exams, project-driven exams, or Web-based testing (under development)

Telling Details

Average Class Load per Instructor
No more than two online courses are taught by any one instructor. This is part of the overall course load.

Faculty Compensation
According to the school, "Faculty are compensated in a different modality. Full-time faculty are evaluated with both on-campus and online courses as equal."

Remote Access to Library?
None

Other Library Resources Available or Recommended
None

Nova Southeastern University

Address

3301 College Avenue
Fort Lauderdale, FL 33314-7796

Phone: (800) 986-3223 Ext. 8550
Fax: (954) 262-3905
E-mail: petinfo@fcae.nova.edu
URL: http:/www.fcae.nova.edu/pet

Contact Person
Vera Flight, Director of Admissions

Description

One of the oldest distance learning Programs, Nova Southeastern prides itself on being the largest school of education in the country and the largest private university in Florida. Based upon a cluster-learning mode, the students and faculty engage in online conversations. Many of the programs are skill based, so the length of the program varies for each student. All students must come to the university three times each year. Nova Southeastern offers programs for professionals who are interested in developing their skills and acquiring advanced degrees. All of the programs are rigorous, requiring intensity and active participation.

Admissions Information

Academic Disciplines
Education, technology, higher education leadership, graduate teacher education program, speech and language pathology

Degrees Offered
M.S. and Ed.D. program in instructional technology and distance education, Ed.D. in educational leadership (K-12, Higher

Education), Graduate Teacher Education Program (GTEP), and Ed.D. in speech and language pathology

Admissions Requirements
Vary according to each program. For example, the requirements for the E.D. in technology are: Current employment as educator or trainer, three years of experience in the field, a bachelor's or master's degree from an accredited institution, access to a computer with modem, experience in Internet and technology use, and demonstrated potential for successful completion of the program.

Equipment Requirements
Computer, modem, Internet access

Tuition and Other Fees
$7,950 per year for doctorate program (3 years is usual time)

Credits Transferable?
Dependent upon college

Overall Program Information

Delivery System
Internet, audiobridge, and polling clusters meeting via computer across country

Year Established
1964

Number of Courses
Varies

Number of Faculty
10–12 in each program

Student Demographics
Educators, media specialists, trainers, computer educators, instructional technologists, curriculum developers, and government and business training specialists

Dropout Rate
Not available, but the school says it is low.

Accreditation
Commission on Colleges of the Southern Associations of Colleges and Schools

Class Information

Average Class Size
25–30

TAs for Large Classes?
No large classes

Length of Session or Semester
Varies according to study area.

Sessions Required for Degree
Requires students to complete multiple study areas (approximately four). Students' skills are assessed upon entry to the program.

Time Commitment per Course
Varies

Participation Expected
Required to participate actively online

Access to Faculty
Phone, online, and compressed video

Grading Procedure
A–F

Testing Procedure
Testing done in area sites and on campus during visits to the university.

Telling Details

Average Class Load per Instructor
1–2 courses

Faculty Compensation
None

Remote Access to Library?
The school library is strong and serves as an important asset to the program. Its catalog is online, and it has access to the Interlibrary Loan system.

Other Library Resources Available or Recommended
In every city where there is a cluster, arrangements have been made with the local library for access

Oklahoma State University

Address

Stillwater, OK 74078

Phone: (405) 744-6876
Fax: (405) 744-5285
E-mail: marshal@okway.okstate.edu
URL: http://mstm-osu@okway.okstate.edu

Contact Person
Marshall Allen
Phone: (405) 744-5960

Description

A long-standing, full-fledged commitment to distance learning permeates Oklahoma State University, which has been delivering telecourses since 1981. High-quality satellite programs are regularly produced in the school's state-of-the-art facilities; courses are also delivered through a fiberoptic system to other locations. Currently there are eight master's degree programs delivered by satellite and supported by both telephone and E-mail. OSU's satellite truck travels around the Midwest delivering programs throughout the world.

Admissions Information

Academic Disciplines
Business, arts and sciences, engineering, and education

Degrees Offered
M.S. in computer science, M.S. in chemical engineering, M.S. in mechanical engineering, M.S. in electrical engineering, M.B.A., Education Specialist in educational administration, M.S. in telecommunications management, M.S. in agriculture

165

Admissions Requirements
Degree from an accredited institution, and GMAT or GRE, depending on the degree program. A background in algebra and educational statistics is required for the M.B.A. program. Students from countries where English isn't spoken must take the TOEFL.

Equipment Requirements
Satellite downlink, computer, and modem

Tuition and Other Fees
Differs according to program; approximately $230 per credit hour

Credits Transferable?
Yes

Overall Program Information

Delivery System
Satellite (real time)

Year Established
1981

Number of Courses
40 per semester

Number of Faculty
50

Student Demographics
Midcareer professionals over 25

Dropout Rate
Very low. Typically the distance-learning students do better than on-campus students in the same class.

Accreditation
North Central Association of Schools and Colleges

Class Information

Average Class Size
30

TAs for Large Classes?
No

Length of Session or Semester
15 weeks

Sessions Required for Degree
30–36 credits

Time Commitment per Course
2 hours for every classroom hour (wide differences in courses and programs)

Participation Expected
All faculty require active participation both in the broadcasts and online.

Access to Faculty
E-mail

Grading Procedure
A–F

Testing Procedure
A facilitator on site proctors examinations. There are also projects to be completed.

Telling Details

Average Class Load per Instructor
2–3 courses (6–9 credit hours)

Faculty Compensation
Faculty receive a percentage of the course net and an "overload" stipend of $50 per student if the class enrollment exceeds the number expected.

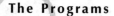
Remote Access to Library?
Oklahoma State University's online library contains much that is full text, all available to the distant student.

Other Library Resources Available or Recommended
Databases and the World Wide Web

PBS Adult Learning Satellite Service

Note: PBS does not award degrees to students directly. See chapter 3 for a description of its offerings.

Address

1320 Braddock Place
Alexandria, VA 22314

Phone: (800) 257-2578
Fax: (703) 739-8492
E-mail: smdavis@pbs.org
URL: http://www.pbs.org

Contact Person
Shirley M. Davis, Associate Director, Adult Learning Service
Phone: (703) 739-5146

Description

A rich treasure house of programs and courses that are given through many universities, some of them for college credit. PBS materials cover the entire range of a liberal arts curriculum, as well as mutiple courses in science, health, and business. PBS courses are licensed to partner institutions, who must provide the satellite downlinks, receivers, and VCRs. Often there is an Internet mail component through the individual college. Plans for the future include "Teleweb" courses.

Admissions Information

Academic Disciplines
A broad spectrum

Degrees Offered
Depends on the partner college.

Admissions Requirements
Depends on the partner college.

Equipment Requirements
The partner college must have a satellite downlink, TV, and VCR

Tuition and Other Fees
Depends on the partner college.

Credits Transferable?
Depends on the partner college.

Program Information

Delivery System
Satellite, broadcast, and the Internet

Year Established
1981

Number of Courses
140 courses and programs

Number of Faculty
Thousands of teachers from a wide variety of institutions.

Student Demographics
There are 400,000 students each year.

Accreditation
Depends on the individual colleges, which are all accredited.

Class Information

Average Class Size
Usually 10–100 per site

Length of Session or Semester
Each video program is approximately 1–2 hours

Sessions Required for Degree
Depends on the partner college

Time Commitment per Course
Varies according to program use

Participation Expected
There are discussions at the colleges after students have viewed the videos.

Access to Faculty
Faculty on video are not available for access.

Grading Procedure
Depends upon the individual college.

Testing Procedure
Depends on the individual college.

Telling Details

Average Class Load per Instructor
Each course reaches thousands of students. College faculty who use these courses varies widely.

Remote Access to Library?
Classes use the library of the partner college, either in person or online.

Other Library Resources Available or Recommended
PBS online, Internet

Pennsylvania State University

Address

Department of Distance Education
211 Mitchell Building
University Park, PA 16802

Phone: (814) 865-5403
Fax: (814) 865-3290
E-mail: psude@cde.psu.edu
URL: http://www.cde.psu.edu/de/

Contact Person
Peter Forster

Description

Distance education at Penn State dates back to correspondence courses that were first established in 1892. Today, distance education is a university-wide function that seeks to create a learner-centered environment characterized by flexibility concerning time, place, and pace of study; a highly interactive experience with faculty and peers; and access to a rich array of resources. The courses are delivered through interactive video to a series of sites around the state, both on other campuses and on-site at corporations.

Admissions Information

Academic Disciplines
Education. Pending are programs are pending in engineering and business.

Degrees Offered
M.Ed.'s in adult education, curriculum and instruction, curriculum and supervision, and counselor education

Admissions Requirements
Same as the requirements for on-campus graduate work

Equipment Requirements
Courses are delivered strictly through interactive video. For future courses, a computer and modem will be necessary for access to the Internet.

Tuition and Other Fees
Depends on the program

Credits Transferable?
Varies

Program Information

Delivery System
Interactive video (real time)

Year Established
The correspondence courses began in 1892.

Total Number of Courses
More than 300

Number of Faculty
200

Dropout Rate
15 percent in the graduate degree program. The rate is somewhat higher among students who are not officially matriculated in the degree program but who are taking graduate-level courses.

Accreditation
Middle States Association of Schools and Colleges

Class Information

Average Class Size
30

TAs for Large Classes?
Yes

Length of Session or Semester
15 weeks

Sessions Required for Degree
36 to 42 semester credit hours

Time Commitment per Course
Three hours per week instruction plus out of class time

Participation Expected
Varies

Access to Faculty
Videoconferencing, E-mail, phone, fax

Grading Procedure
A–F

Testing Procedure
Proctored exams or papers

Telling Details

Average Class Load per Instructor
1

Faculty Compensation
No

Remote Access to Library?
Yes

Other Library Resources Available or Recommended
No

Purdue University

Address

Continuing Engineering Education
1575 Civil Engineering Building, Room G216
West Lafayette, IN 47907

Phone: (765) 494-7015
Fax: (765) 496-1196
E-mail: cee@ecn.purdue.edu
URL: http://cee.www.ecn.purdue.edu/cee/

Contact Person
Ask for the program director when calling or writing.

Description

Graduate courses in engineering and related disciplines are tele-vised live as they are taught on the West Lafayette campus by Purdue's engineering faculty. These courses may be taken on a cred-it or audit basis. Qualified engineers may apply for admission to the Graduate School of Purdue University and, upon admission, work toward one of several master's degrees, which may be earned entirely through televised courses.

Admissions Information

Academic Disciplines
Engineering

Degrees Offered
Master of Science, Master of Science in engineering, Master of Science in electrical engineering, Master of Science in industrial engineering, Master of Science in mechanical engineering

Admissions Requirements
These vary according to the master's degree sought. All applicants should have a bachelor's degree in engineering or a closely aligned subject and an undergraduate GPA of at least 3.0.

Equipment Requirements
Vary depending upon the course.

Tuition and Other Fees
For delivery via IHETS (see "Delivery System" below) or the Internet, Indiana residents pay $579 per 3 credit hour course and nonresidents pay $1,314 per 3-credit course. For delivery via videotape, Indiana residents pay $1,268 per 3-credit course and nonresidents pay $1,488 per 3-credit course. There is also a $8 technology fee per semester and a $30 one-time application fee.

Credits Transferable?
Up to 12 credits from other accredited schools

Program Information

Delivery System
The Indiana Higher Education Telecommunication System (IHETS), a satellite television network (real time delivery is optional). Indiana University also produces some National Technological University courses via satellite. Other courses are delivered via videotape and the Internet.

Year Established
1967

Total Number of Courses
Approximately 160

Number of Faculty
More than 75

Student Demographics
Working adults from the United States and other countries.

Accreditation
North Central Association of Colleges and Schools

Class Information

Average Class Size
Thirty off-campus students (in addition to on-campus class)

TAs for Large Classes?
Yes

Length of Session or Semester
Each semester is 16 weeks long and consists of either 40, 50-minute sessions or 33, 75-minute sessions.

Sessions Required for Degree
Thirty semester credit hours (typical load: three credit hours per session)

Time Commitment per Course
Varies. The minimum is nine hours per week for 16 weeks (two hours outside class for each hour in class)

Participation Expected
Varies by course. Minimal participation is typical.

Access to Faculty
Primarily telephone, fax, E-mail, World Wide Web

Grading Procedure
The traditional 4.0 scale is used. The grade is determined by the course professor.

Testing Procedure
Determined by the course professor

Telling Details

Average Class Load per Instructor
One to two courses per semester

Faculty Compensation
Yes

Remote Access to Library
Via the Internet or dial-up access using a computer and modem, allowing distance-learning students the same access to online databases as on-campus students have

Other Library Resources Available or Recommended
For library materials that are not available at a local library, the staff at Purdue's Technical Information Service (TIS) can locate and send the materials at a reasonable cost.

Queens University

Address

Kingston, Ontario K-7L
3N6
Canada

Phone: (613) 545-6811
Fax: (613) 545-2313
E-mail: nemba@qsilver.queensu.ca
URL: http://www.execmba.com

Contact Person
Dr. Donald Nightingale, Executive Director

Description

With more than 155 entrants and more than 200 ongoing participants, the program at Queens University is the largest M.B.A. program in Canada. Senior level managers study at their work site or at rooms set up by the telephone company and the government through interactive multipoint videoconferencing. There are presently 23 in Canada and Bermuda used for the two-year master's degree. Students meet on Friday and Saturday morning at the sites for instruction. There is a high residency requirement for this program—five weeks in all: two each August and one before graduation. There is also an international two-week study trip. The program is comprehensive and well-developed with a high acceptance factor throughout Canada.

Admissions Information

Academic Disciplines
Business

Degrees Offered
M.B.A.

Admissions Requirements
Any three of the following four requirements: An undergraduate degree with good standing, senior management experience or potential, Good GMAT or QMAT (Canadian equivalent) scores, and outstanding references

Equipment Requirements
Computer, modem, and Internet access are included in the tuition. Travel and accommodations during residencies are also included.

Tuition and Other Fees
$52,000 Canadian (2 years, all inclusive)

Credits Transferable
No

Program Information

Delivery System
Videoconferencing

Year Established
1994

Total Number of Courses
22

Number of Faculty
30

Student Demographics
Most students are mid- to upper-level professionals with nine years of management experience and 15 years of work experience. The average age is 43. Thirty percent of the students are female.

Dropout Rate
No exact data; very low. Many of those who leave the program are deferring and not dropping out.

Accreditation
The program is accredited by the university

Class Information

Average Class Size
75

TAs for Large Classes?
Graders, tutors, and team facilitators are a part of each class and course.

Length of Session or Semester
There are continuous sessions from September to May. Different courses are different lengths--there can be 4, 6, 8, or 12 sessions lasting three and a half hours each.

Sessions Required for Degree
22 months

Time Commitment per Course
20–25 hours per week, including the class time

Participation Expected
This is a very participative program. There are learning teams and a great deal of group work.

Access to Faculty
Students and faculty communicate through Execmba Online, their Internet Connection.

Grading Procedure
No traditional grades.

Testing Procedure
There are projects and assignments.

Telling Details

Average Class Load per Instructor
There are usually two courses per instructor. One distance-learning course could fulfill 75 percent of the course load.

Faculty Compensation
Faculty receive additional pay for distance-learning courses.
Teaching is essential to tenure decisions.

Remote Access to Library?
Yes—Queens Library

Other Library Resources Available or Recommended
World Wide Web, Internet

Rensselaer Polytechnic Institute

Address

Rensselaer Satellite Video Program (RSVP)
Office of Continuing and Distance Education
CII Suite 4011
Troy, NY 12180

Phone: (518) 276-6789
Fax: (518) 276-8026
Email: grad-services@rpi.edu
URL: http://www.rpi.edu

Contact Person
Kim Scalzo
Phone: (518) 276-8351

Description

One of the most prestigious engineering colleges in the country, RPI delivers many master's programs via distance learning, through several different systems. It is possible to receive a degree at many corporate sites at which RPI has a relationship. This program is based closely on the equivalent program on campus; in fact, in many cases, both the on-campus population and the off-site learners interact on a regular basis. Faculty teach both groups as part of their teaching load.

Admissions Information

Academic Disciplines
Engineering, business

Degrees Offered
M.S. in engineering, M.S. in management and technology, MBA, M.S. in microelectronics manufacturing engineering, Master of

Engineering in manufacting systems engineering, M.S. in engineering information systems reliability, M.S. in mechanical engineering

Admissions Requirements
Transcript, degree from an accredited university, application, and two letters of recommendation

Equipment Requirements
Satellite downlink, videoconferencing room, VCR, computer, modem

Tuition and Other Fees
$600 per credit hour

Credits Transferable?
Contact advisor for information on transferability

Program Information

Delivery Systems
Videoconferencing, videotape, satellite TV

Year Established
1987

Total Number of Courses
Approximately 14 per semester

Number of Faculty
14 each semester

Student Demographics
Middle-level professionals in corporations

Dropout Rate
Very low

Accreditation
New England Associaton of Schools and Colleges

Class Information

Average Class Size
10–60

TAs for large classes?
Yes

Length of Session or Semester
15 weeks

Sessions Required for Degree
30–36 credits

Time Commitment per Course
10–20 hours

Participation Expected
Personal contact is expected at all times, regardless of the delivery system

Access to Faculty
E-mail, phone, fax

Grading Procedure
A–F

Testing Procedure
Proctors at corporate sites administer the tests

Telling Details

Average Class Load per Instructor
2

Faculty Compensation
Yes

Remote Access to Library?
Access to a video library and the Internet

Other Library Resources Available or Recommended
Databases and e-mail distribution lists on the Web

Rochester Institute of Technology

Address

91 Lomb Memorial Drive
Rochester NY 14623

Phone: (800) CALL-RIT or (716) 475-5089
Fax: (716) 475-5077
E-mail: ritdl@rit.edu
URL: http://www.rit.edu

Admissions Information

Academic Disciplines
Applied science and technology (both areas comprise one discipline)

Degrees Offered
M.S. in software development and management; M.S. in information technology; M.S. in health systems adminstration; M.S. in environmental, health and safety management (new in 1997–98); and graduate certificates in statistical quality, integrated health systems, and finance for health systems

Admissions Requirements
Vary by academic department. Basic requirement is a completed baccalaureate or equivalent degree from an accredited institution with a minimum GPA of 3.0.

Equipment Requirements
Video playback in TV monitor, computer (see the hardware requirements below), Internet connectivity, telephone. Hardware requirements: minimum 8 MB of RAM (16 MB preferred, 32 MB suggested); 20 MB of available hard drive space, 14.4 modem (28.8 preferred), and Windows 95/NT, Windows 3.1, or Macintosh System 7.1 or higher.

Tuition and Other Fees
$253 per credit hour

Credits Transferable?
Depends upon program

Program Information

Delivery System
Videotape, online (both E-mail and real-time chat rooms)

Year Established
1979

Number of Courses
140

Number of Faculty
More than 100

Student Demographics
Primarily adult, part-time students

Dropout Rate
None reported

Accreditation
Middle States Association of States and Colleges

Class Information

Average Class Size
22

TAs for Large Classes?
As needed

Length of Session or Semester
11-week quarter

Sessions Required for Degree
Varies by program

Time Commitment per Course
At least 40 hours for a four-credit course

Participation Expected
High participation and interaction required for most courses

Access to Faculty
E-mail and telephone

Grading Procedure
Varies by course

Testing Procedure
Varies by course

Telling Details

Average Class Load per Instructor
Same as on campus

Faculty Compensation
Yes

Remote Access to Library?
Yes

Other Library Resources Available or Recommended
Yes

Salve Regina University

Address

100 Ochre Point Avenue
Newport, RI 02840-4192

Phone: (401) 847-6650, ext. 2229
Fax: (401) 847-0372
E-mail: mistoe@aol.com
URL: http:// www.salve.edu

Contact Person
Sister Leona Mistoe

Description

Distance learning has been part of Salve Regina for many years. The old Naval War College was in Newport, and the navy seamen took master's programs both onsite and while out to sea. The technology was strictly pencil and paper in those days: In recent years, technological advancements have led the university to analyze its offerings and make certain courses available online. The university still stresses the human element; all students are assigned an advisor and meet online with their advisors at least three times during each course. This is a highly individualized program. The entire degree is one student working with one faculty member. Initially they design the course of study together.

Admissions Information

Academic Disciplines
International relations, human development and management

Degrees Offered
M.A. in human development
M.A. in international relations
M.S. in management (regular management, correctional institutions, or insurance)

Admissions Requirements
Degree from an accredited college and GRE, MAT, or LSAT

Equipment Requirements
Computer and modem. If these are unavailable (as in correctional institutions), pencil and paper will suffice.

Tuition and Other Fees
$900 per course, $100–200 book fee, $35 application fee, $100 commitment fee

Credits Transferable?
Yes: six credits can be transfered to a degree awarding institution and 12–18 can be transfered to an institution that doesn't award degrees (Army or Navy War College, for example)

Overall Program Information

Delivery System
All asynchronous online or via mail

Year Established
1983

Number of Courses
40

Number of Faculty
40

Student Demographics
No demographic records; mostly midcareer military or business executives. There are many foreign officers interested in a United States degree.

Dropout Rate
Under 10 percent. Most students need only a few courses to complete a degree because of liberal transfer policy.

Accreditation
New England Association of Schools and Colleges

Class Information

Average Class Size
All individual, with one student per teacher.

TAs for Large Classes?
Not applicable

Length of Session or Semester
6 months

Sessions Required for Degree
36 credits

Time Commitment per Course
Completely individualized program

Participation Expected
Depends upon individual commitments and faculty expectations

Access to Faculty
E-mail

Grading Procedure
A–F

Testing Procedure
Either proctored exams, an open-book exam, or a research paper

Telling Details

Average Class Load per Instructor
15 students at any one time

Faculty Compensation
All faculty are treated as adjuncts for distance courses even if they are full time on campus. No credit toward tenure is given for a distance learning program.

Remote Access to Library?
Through the Web to Salve Regina Library

Other Library Resources Available or Recommended
All necessary resources are sent to each individual.

Southern Methodist University

Address

School of Engineering and Applied Science (SEAS)
PO Box 750335
Dallas TX 75275-0335

Phone: (800) 601-4040
Fax: (214) 768-3778
E-mail: sdye@seas.smu.edu
URL: http://www.seas.smu.edu

Contact Person
Stephanie Dye, Associate Director, Distance Education

Description

Southern Methodist University was founded in 1911. SMU's School of Engineering and Applied Science provides distance learning programs via a worldwide videotape program, through the National Technological University, and via the North Texas TAGER microwave network. The videotape program reaches students at corporations in all parts of the nation and at military bases in the United States and overseas. A $1.2 million upgrade to new, state-of-the-art studio classrooms took place in the summer of 1997.

Admissions Information

Academic Disciplines
Engineering and applied science

Degrees Offered
Master's degrees in telecommunications, engineering management, systems engineering, manufacturing systems, hazardous and waste materials management, and software engineering.

Admissions Requirements
A bachelor's degree in science or engineering and GPA of 3.0

Equipment Requirements
Television, VCR, computer, modem

Tuition and Other Fees
$630 per credit hour (most courses are three credits)

Credits Transferable
6 hours of transfer credit

Program Information

Delivery System
Videotapes

Year Established
1964 (videotapes)

Number of Courses
120

Number of Faculty
55

Student Demographics
Military personnel from around the world and corporate working professionals. About 30 percent are women. The ages of students range fro 25–45

Dropout Rate
10–15 percent

Accreditation
Southern Association of Colleges and Schools

Class Information

Average Class Size
15–20

TAs for Large Classes?
No

Length of Session or Semester
15 weeks

Sessions Required for Degree
30–36 semester credits with a minimum of a 3.0 GPA

Time Commitment per Course
Students are expected to spend two to three times the duration of the classroom video instruction in their studies.

Participation Expected
No active participation—there are only lectures and individual research projects

Access to Faculty
Mostly E-mail, some telephone, and fax

Grading Procedure
A–F

Testing Procedure
Staff at the site distributes and proctors all exams. They are sent to the professor for grading.

Telling Details

Average Class Load per Instructor
Same as on campus; virtually all graduate classes are used for distance education.

TAs for Large Classes?
Rebroadcasts do not require extra persons to act as TAs.

Faculty Compensation
There is no difference between on- and off-campus pay.

Remote Access to Library?
Special requests are handled by the library. There is no regular access by students.

Other Library Resources Available or Recommended
Web site

Stanford University

Address

Stanford Center for Professional Development
401 Durand Building
Stanford, CA 94305-4036

Phone: (650) 725-3000
Fax: (650) 725-2868
E-mail: scpd@forsythe.edu
URL: http://scpd.stanford.edu

Contact Person
Carolyn Schultz
Phone: (650) 725-3000

Description

The Honors Cooperative Program (HCP) is Stanford's only part-time graduate program. It allows working professionals to earn a graduate engineering degree by utilizing the latest technologies. Master's degrees are given in both engineering and computer science. There are also professional executive programs, consisting of ten courses in business management and leadership. Stanford has been researching applications of communications technologies, working with the computer industry, its student body, and those interested in distance learning from companies within a 35-mile radius. A three-month residency is required to obtain a degree.

Admissions Information

Academic Disciplines
Engineering, business, and computer science

Degrees Offered
Master's programs in engineering and computer science, graduate courses, certificate program

Admissions Requirements
The same highly selective admissions procedures for Stanford are used in the distance-learning programs.

Equipment Requirements
Depending on program, VCR, computer, corporate facilities for compressed video, microwave transmission, Vxtreme plug-in for Windows 95/NT

Tuition and Other Fees
$922 per unit for degree student, $670 per unit for nondegree student

Credits Transferable?
Depends on institution; up to 15 credits

Overall Program Information

Delivery System
Microwave transmission, tutored videotape, two-way compressed video, Asynchronous Distance Learning Project (Stanford Online)

Year Established
1969

Number of Courses
225

Number of Faculty
150

Student Demographics
Students employed in technology industries

Accreditation
Western Association of Schools and Colleges

Class Information

Average Class Size
15 off-campus students combined with onsite class

TAs for Large Classes?
Yes

Length of Session or Semester
Quarter system 30 hours each quarter

Sessions Required for Degree
15

Time Commitment per Course
Two to three times each class hour is the minimum.

Participation Expected
Some courses require active participation (those in real time). Other faculty require some online conversations. The variety depends on faculty.

Access to Faculty
E-mail

Grading Procedure
A–F

Testing Procedure
A liaison administers tests at industry sites.

Telling Details

Average Class Load per Instructor
1 class

Faculty Compensation
Yes. There is also a three-way licensing agreement if the faculty member leaves: Compensation is divided equally among the professor, the department, and the school.

Remote Access to Library?
No. Some Interlibrary Loan arrangements are possible.

Other Library Resources Available or Recommended
No.

Stephens College

Address
College of Graduate and Continuing Education
Campus Box 2083
Columbia, MO 65215

Phone: (800) 388-7579
Fax: (573) 446-6072
E-mail: grad@wc.stephens.edu
URL: http://www.stephens.edu

Contact Person
Dr. Joan Rines, director

Description

The second-oldest women's college in the United States, Stephens has served both male and female students through its School of Continuing Education since 1971. This online M.B.A. is geared towards working professionals committed to pursuing a graduate-level degree while maintaining their current job and residence. Two campus visits are required, one for a first-year weekend workshop, one for the program's capstone course; the rest is delivered online. Online students are encouraged to interact both with the faculty and their fellow students in a dynamic exchange of ideas and information.

Admissions Information

Class Information
Business administration

Degrees Offered
M.B.A.

Admissions Requirements
GMAT score combined with undergraduate GPA are given primary consideration in the acceptance decision. A minimum GPA of 3.0 in the last 60 hours of undergraduate work is required.

Equipment Requirements
Computer with reliable Internet access

Tuition and Other Fees
$230 per credit hour

Credits Transferable?
Up to nine credit hours may be transferred, subject to approval by program director

Program Information

Delivery System
Online. Students must also make two required campus visits.

Year Established
1997

Number of Courses
26

Number of Faculty
Currently six; college plans to increase this number to around 12 as the program grows to its expected size

Student Demographics
This is a new program, so statistics are not yet available. From advance research, however, the college expects program partici-pants to have between 5 and 25 years of work experience, and to reside throughout the United States as well as in other countries. A majority of participants are expected to be women but many men will also apply and be accepted.

Accreditation
North Central Association of Colleges and Schools

Class Information

Average Class Size
Not available

TAs for Large Classes?
No—Stephens has no TAs.

Length of Session or Semester
Four ten-week sessions per year

Sessions Required for Degree
36 minimum semester hours

Time Commitment per Course
Students are expected to spend ten to twelves hours per week, which includes time in communications with other participants both in and out of class.

Participation Expected
This will vary somewhat by professor. Typically, students might be expected to be in contact weekly with professors regarding assignments and will be expected to participate weekly in the electronic discussions via listserve

Access to Faculty
E-mail and telephone

Grading Procedure
Will vary by professor; in general, will probably be a combination of exams, case studies or other papers, homework, and participation. There would be no diferentiation between local and non-local students.

Testing Procedure
A proctor in the student's area will administer the exams and ensure the integrity of the exams

Telling Details

Average Class Load per Instructor
Still to be determined; average class size and numbers in the program will influence this.

Faculty Compensation
Yes

Remote Access to Library
Yes

Other Library Resources Available or Recommended
Course materials to be available on faculty Web sites. These may include syllabi, assignment instructions, cases studies, work of other/previous students, links to related Web sites, etcetera.

Stevens Institute of Technology

Address

Castle Point on Hudson
Hoboken, NJ 07030

Phone: (201) 216-5000
Fax: (201)216-8044
E-mail: thegradschool@stevens-tech.edu
URL: http://www.stevens-tech.edu

Contact Person
Joseph J. Moeller, Jr.
Phone: *(201) 216-5229*
E-mail: jmoeller@stevens-tech.edu

Description

Stevens Institute of Technology offers graduate degree and continuing professional development programs in a distance learning environment, primarily through video conferencing technologies. Using this medium, both local and remote students have the ability to fully interact with each other and with the instructor-mentor in real time. To supplement the video-based setting, Stevens uses Internet-based asynchronous communications (E-mail, conferencing, etcetera) between instructors and students. These distance-learning programs are arranged through partnership or collaboration with business and industry. The students are employees of companies with which such distance learning activities are arranged.

Admissions Information

Academic Disciplines
Management, project management, human factors, computer science, telecommunications management, electrical engineering.

Degrees Offered
Master of Science, Master of Engineering, Graduate Certificate of
Special Study (credit-bearing)

Admissions Requirements
Baccalaureate degree, application, and letters of recommendation

Equipment Requirements
Access to videoconferencing facility (CoDEC, camera, monitor,
ISDN communication line)

Tuition and Other Fees
$650 per credit for 1997–98, $45 application fee, $75 per semester
enrollment fee

Credits Transferable?
Stevens accepts up to 10 credits transferred toward a 30-credit
master's degree from Stevens

Program Information

Delivery System
Interactive video (real-time) supplemented with computer-based
communications

Year Established
1994

Number of Courses
40

Number of Faculty
12

Student Demographics
Students in New Jersey, Florida, Colorado, Massachusetts, and
Kansas

Dropout Rate
2 percent

Accreditation
Middle States Association of Colleges and Schools, Accrediting Board for Engineering and Technology (ABET), and Computer Science Accrediting Board (CSAB).

Class Information

Length of Session or Semester
Five weeks per course

Sessions Required for Degree
12 courses for the master's degree; four to seven courses for Graduate Certificate of Special Study

Time Commitment per Course
2.5 hours per week

Participation Expected
Full participation as would be expected from a graduate student: class participation, assignments, case studies, examinations

Access to Faculty
Interactive video, phone, E-mail, and fax

Grading Procedure
Varies by course

Testing Procedure
Varies by course

Telling Details

Average Class Load per Instructor
Two or three courses per semester

Faculty Compensation
Yes

Remote Access to Library
Yes

Other Library Resources Available or Recommended
Yes

Syracuse University

Address

4-206 Center for Science and Technology
Syracuse, NY 13244-4100

Phone: (315) 443-2911
Fax: (315) 4435806
E-mail: ist@syr.edu
URL: http://istweb.syr.edu

Contact Person
Amy Merrill, Director of Distance Education
Phone: (315) 443-4251
E-mail: almerrill@syr.edu

Description

The School of Information Studies specializes in innovative programs in information policy, information behavior, information management, information systems, information technology, and information services. Among the professional degree programs the school offers is a distance education program featuring two degrees--a Master in Library Science and a Master in Information Resources Management. The school's curriculum focuses on the information needs of users as a starting point for integrating information and information technology into organizations.

The faculty combines expertise in information systems, linguistics, computer science, library science, business management, management information systems, telecommunications, and communication.

Admissions Information

Academic Disciplines
Library science, business

Degrees Offered
Master of Library Science, Master of Information Resources Management

Admissions Requirements
A completed application, letters of recommendation, a statement of goals, and GRE scores

Equipment Requirements
Computer with Internet access

Tuition and Other Fees
$529 per credit hour

Credits Transferable?
6 credits transferable with approval

Overall Program Information

Delivery System
Online delivery

Year Established
1991–1994

Number of Courses
26

Number of Faculty
5 full-time plus adjuncts

Student Demographics
Both in-state and international

Dropout Rate
Very low

Accreditation
Amerian Library Association

Class Information

Average Class Size
25–30

TAs for Large Classes?
Yes

Length of Session or Semester
Five to six months

Sessions Required for Degree
36 credit hours

Time Commitment per Course
The norm is 2–3 hours per class hour

Participation Expected
High level of individual participation

Access to Faculty
E-mail, phone

Grading Procedure
A–F

Testing Procedure
Projects and proctored tests

Telling Details

Average Class Load per Instructor
1–2

Faculty Compensation
Yes

Remote Access to Library?
Yes

Other Library Resources Available or Recommended
Databases, World Wide Web

Thomas Edison
State College

Address

101 West State Street
Trenton, NJ 08608-1176

Phone: (609) 984-1150
Fax: (609) 984-8447
E-mail: admissions@call.tesc.edu
URL: http://www.tesc.edu

Description

Thomas Edison offers an extensive array of distance-learning courses at the undergraduate level, thanks to its Computer-Assisted Lifelong Learning (CALL) Network, which functions as an online community for students both on and off campus. In January 1996, the College launched its first graduate program—the Master of Science in Management—in conjunction with AT&T. The first MSM class graduated in the summer of 1997, and consisted mostly of AT&T managers. It is a two-year, 36-credit program that is designed to provide a rigorous educational experience for seasoned managers who show promise for growth and advancement in their organizational roles. The program is built on a cohort model—students are admitted together and move through the program as a group. Three residencies are required: a weekend orientation and two extended residencies of five to seven days. Thomas Edison expects MSM students to be supported by their employers, including offering either full or partial payment of costs.

Admissions Information

Academic Disciplines
Management

Degrees Offered
Master of Science in management

Admissions Requirements
Undergraduate degree from an accredited college or university and demonstrated competence in the professional world. Candidates must be motivated and self-directed with a proven knowledge in management-related areas and an ability to write with clarity and purpose.

Equipment Requirements
Computer with a 486 CPU of 33 MHz or faster; 8 MB RAM; 14.4 modem; Internet access including a Web browser and E-mail account

Tuition and Other Fees
$289 per credit hour; $75 nonrefundable application fee, and an estimated $150 per course in books, software, and other study materials. Students will be expected to pay travel, accommodations, and materials costs for the residencies, estimated at $500 for the orientation weekend and $1,000 each for the other two residencies

Credits Transferable?
Students who have successfully completed graduate-level course work in business or management at a regionally accredited college or university, or through corporate courses evaluated by the American Council on Education, may request a review to waive the six required hours of elective courses.

Program Information

Delivery System
Online. Three residency periods are also required.

Year Established
1996

Number of Courses
12

Number of Faculty
36

Student Demographics
The average age is 42, with a range between 28 and 60. Most students are mid- to senior-level managers. There is a 50-50 male-female ratio. Minorities comprise 25 percent of the enrollment. Students reside in nine different states.

Dropout Rate
2 percent

Accreditation
Middle States Association of Colleges and Schools

Class Information

Average Class Size
16

TAs for Large Classes?
No

Length of Session or Semester

Sessions Required for Degree
42 semester hours, completed in seven consecutive semesters

Time Commitment per Course
Depends upon the student's learning style.

Participation Expected
Students are expected to attend all the residencies and take all of the courses and exams.

Access to Faculty
E-mail, phone

Grading Procedure
Each course is graded with an A, B, C, or No Credit

Testing Procedure
Final exams and/or course projects and case studies

Telling Details

Average Class Load per Instructor
Each instructor teaches one class per term.

Faculty Compensation
Yes

Remote Access to Library
Students have access to the entire state library system, which is administered by Thomas Edison College.

Other Library Resources Available or Recommended
Students also access local libraries, links, through college Web site

Union Institute

Address

440 East McMillan Street
Cincinnati, OH 45226

Phone: (513) 861-6400 or (800) 486-3116
Fax: (513) 861-0779
E-mail   gradoff@tui.edu
URL: http://www.tui.edu

Contact Person
Michael J. Robertson, Associate Registrar, Admissions
Phone: (513) 861-6400 or (800) 486-3116
Fax: (513) 861-0779
E-mail   mrobertson@tui.edu

Description

The Union Institute is a private university that has provided flexible, individualized, learner-initiated degree programs exclusively for adults since 1964. The school's focus is on blending academics with real-world experience, emphasizing the practical application of learning rather than memorization. The Union Institute's educational system is designed for those who have the motivation and ability to assume a significant measure of personal responsibility for planning and executing their degree programs. Each program is built upon previous learning and is designed to engage the student (the school prefers to use the word *learner*) with a wide variety of learning resources and experiences. Faculty mentors work closely with students to provide guidance and evaluation of their progress.

Admissions Information

Academic Disciplines
Interdisciplinary studies in the liberal arts and sciences, clinical psychology

Degrees Offered
Doctor of Philosophy (Ph.D.)

Admissions Requirements
Master's degree from a regionally accredited institution, completed and signed application, three narrative essays, three letters of recommendation, and official transcripts.

Equipment Requirements
There are no equipment requirements, but Internet access is recommended.

Admissions Requirements
Tuition for 1997–98 is $4,090 per semester. There is also a $50 nonrefundable application fee

Program Information

Delivery System
All graduate programs are individually designed and independently executed doctoral programs, so the delivery systems are determined, to a great extent, by each learner. There is a brief (35-day total) residency requirement consisting of a 10-day entry colloquium, three 5-day seminars, and 10 single-day miniseminars (peer days). Students must also attend monthly colloquiums held at locations throughout the United States. Seminars are generally conducted in person, with a few conducted online (though not in real time). Students can attend peer days either in person or online. Contact with faculty, administration, and other learners takes place in-person or by phone, fax, E-mail, and regular mail.

Year Established
Founded in 1964 as the Union for Experimenting Colleges and Universities (UECU), The Union Institute awarded its first doctoral degree in 1971.

Number of Courses
In addition to 22 colloquiums, the Graduate College offers approximately 60 seminars each year. Each seminar is described in detail in an annual catalog.

Number of Faculty

There are, at present, 85 Graduate College faculty serving as advisors on students' doctoral committees. In addition, Graduate College students select two non–Union Institute adjunct faculty to serve on the doctoral committee. This selection takes place in consultation with the faculty advisor.

Student Demographics

The total Graduate College enrollment is 1,249. Of those, 42 percent are men and 58 percent are women. The average age is 46. The enrollment is 69.3 percent white, 14.8 percent black, 3.0 percent Hispanic, 1.8 percent Asian American and Pacific Islander, and 1.4 percent American Indian and Native Alaskan. The ethnicity of 7.9 percent of the enrollment is unknown. Students live in 48 states, Puerto Rico, the United States Virgin Islands, and 17 countries around the world.

Dropout Rate

15 percent withdrew in 1990–91; 14 percent in 1991–92; 16 percent in 1992–93, 11 percent in 1993–94; 7 percent in 1994–95; 6 percent in 1995–96; and 4 percent in 1996–97.

Accreditation

The Union Institute holds full membership (accredited) status with the Commission on Institutions of Higher Education of the North Central Association of Colleges and Schools

Class Information

Average Class Size

The College's residency component requires students to participate in one 10-day entry colloquium (limited to 20 students, with two instructors—known as "conveners" in Union Institute parlance), and three 5-day seminars (time, location, and topic of the student's choice). Seminar sizes vary, typically with 15 to 20 Graduate College students and two faculty conveners.

Length of Session or Semester

Graduate College students enroll annually and pay tuition by semester, but the program itself is not driven by semesters. Students matriculate and graduate each month.

Sessions Required for Degree

A minimum of 24 months of full-time enrollment is required for graduation.

Time Commitment per Course

Graduate College programs are self-paced.

Access to Faculty

Graduate College faculty may be accessed in person or by telephone, E-mail, or regular mail.

Grading Procedure

The awarding of equivalent graduate semester credits requires at least B-level achievement.

Testing Procedure

Students are assessed individually using written and oral products and other demonstrations of competency.

Telling Details

Average Class Load

Graduate College faculty serve as core advisors to no more than 25 doctoral students.

Faculty Compensation

Not applicable. Since distance learning comprises the entire graduate program, there is no special compensation structure. The Union Institute has no tenure system.

Remote Access to Library

Yes, via The Union Institute's Internet homepage. The campus library collection is limited to doctoral dissertations of Union Institute graduates.

Other Library Resources Available or Recommended

Yes. Students are encouraged to seek as many resources as possible in conducting their doctoral research. The Union Institute provides online access, via its Internet homepage, to a variety of library collections and has a full-time staff member to assist students with online research.

University of Alabama

Address

College of Continuing Studies
Division of Distance Education
127 Martha Parham West
Box 870388
Tuscaloosa, AL 35487-0388

Phone: (205) 348-5991
Fax: (205) 348-8816
E-mail: jdoss@ccs.ua.edu

Contact Person
Jennifer Doss

Description

At the graduate level, the University of Alabama offers distance - learning courses through one of two programs (in addition to being one of the institutions providing courses for National Technological University). One is a program called Quality University Extended Site Telecourse, or QUEST, which delivers classes via videotape to a student's workplace or to a QUEST site, of which there are now 264 internationally. QUEST courses are regular University courses which are videotaped in special studio-classrooms. The other program is called the Interactive Intercampus Telecommunication System (IITS). This is a network of conference rooms connected by compressed-video technology, and available only at one of 22 IITS sites in Alabama. The University appears proud of its distance-learning programs but did not provide much in the way of details that readers of this book might find informative.

Admissions Information

Class Information
QUEST: aerospace engineering, environmental engineering, electrical engineering, mechanical engineering, engineering

IITS: tax law, advertising and public relations, rehabilitation counseling, health studies

Degrees Offered
M.S., M.A.

Admissions Requirements
Same as on campus students

Equipment Requirements
QUEST: access to a TV and VCR
IITS: provided at IITS sites

Tuition and Other Fees
QUEST: $157.50 per semester hour, plus $25 registration free each semester
IITS: same as on campus

Credits Transferable?
Yes

Program Information

Delivery System
QUEST: videotape. IITS: two-way videoconferencing (real time)

Year Established
1991 (both QUEST and IITS)

Total Number of Courses
Varies

Number of Faculty
Varies

Student Demographics
QUEST: international. IITS: Alabama residents

Dropout Rate
Not tracked

Accreditation
Southern Association of Schools and Colleges

Class Information

Average Class Size
Varies

TAs for Large Classes?
Varies

Length of Session or Semester
Same as on campus

Sessions Required for Degree
Varies

Time Commitment per Course
Same as on campus

Participation Expected
QUEST: no direct interaction. IITS: same as on campus

Access to Faculty
E-mail and telephone

Grading Procedure
Same as on campus

Testing Procedure
Same as on campus

Telling Details

Average Class Load per Instructor
Varies

Faculty Compensation
Yes

Remote Access to Library
Yes

Other Library Resources Available or Recommended
Yes

University of California— Santa Barbara

Address

Off-Campus Studies
University of California, Santa Barbara
Santa Barbara, CA 93106

Phone: (805) 893-4056
Fax: (805) 893-8124
E-mail: ocs2domi@ucsbvm.ucsb.edu
URL: http://www.ucsb.edu

Contact Person
Marcus Domingus

Description

Classes are televised live to Ventura Center, joining two campuses. The program allows an extension of the campus that is available to non-traditional students, particularly those in corporations, government, or in the military. While not as extensive as other California programs, this has been a successful implementation of distance learning on a small scale. Undoubtedly it will grow to encompass other technologies.

Admissions Information

Academic Disciplines
Engineering

Degrees Offered
Master's in electrical and computer engineering, M.S. in computer science

Admissions Requirements
A degree from an accredited institution, GPA of 3.0, GRE

Equipment Requirements
Access to classroom, VCR, television, computer lab, home or office computer

Tuition and Other Fees
$3,900 per year (3 quarters)

Credits Transferable
12 units

Program Information

Delivery System
Interactive audio and video, videotapes

Year Established
1978

Number of Courses
8 per quarter, 24 each year

Number of Faculty
24

Student Demographics
Regular graduate students who already have an engineering undergraduate degree. Many work at corporation who participate in the program. Large numbers come from the military. Twenty percent are women. Students range from 30–35 years old.

Dropout Rate
The dropout rate is very low because selection is careful. Many who want to attend are rejected.

Accreditation
Western Association of Schools and Colleges

Class Information

Average Class Size
4–5

TAs for Large Classes?
All TAs are located on campus.

Length of Session or Semester
10 weeks

Sessions Required for Degree
42 quarter units

Time Commitment per Course
12–16 hours

Participation Expected
Little participation is necessary. The program is lecture based with some computer assignments

Access to Faculty
E-mail and telephone office hours

Grading Procedure
A–F

Testing Procedure
There are written essays, projects, a midterm at the Ventura Center, and a final exam that must be taken on campus.

Telling Details

Average Class Load per Instructor
1–2 courses

Faculty Compensation
Faculty receive an additional stipend.

Remote Access to Library?
Yes

Other Library Resources Available or Recommended
There is a daily courier service between the two campuses.

University of Florida

Address—Business Administration Program

Warrington College of Business Administration
134 Bryan Hall
P.O. Box 117152
Gainesville, FL 32611-7152

Phone: (352) 392-7992 X 1200
Fax: (352) 392-8791
E-mail: ufmba@dale.cba.ufl.edu
URL: http://www.cba.ufl.edu/mba

Contact Person
Dr. T. Craig Tapley
Director, Florida M.B.A. Programs
ctapley@notes.cba.ufl.edu

Address—Engineering Program

College of Engineering
Outreach Engineering Education Program (OEEP)
P.O. Box 116100
Gainesville, FL 32611

Phone: (352) 392-9670
Fax: (352) 846-2255
E-mail: feeds@eng.ufl.edu
URL: http://www.eng.ufl.edu/oeep

Contact Person
Arthur J. Zirger, Jr.
E-mail: azirg@eng.ufl.edu

Address—Pharmacy Program

College of Pharmacy
Box 100484, JHMHC
Gainesville, FL 32610

Phone: (352) 392-9714
Fax: (352) 392-3480
E-mail: robinson@cop.health.ufl.edu
URL: http://www.cop.ufl.edu/wppd

Description

The University of Florida has three distinct schools offering distance learning programs: the Warrington College of Business Administration, the College of Engineering, and the College of Pharmacy. (Additionally, the University offers one graduate-level A*DEC course.) These programs are not gathered under any one administrative office; contact whichever individual school in which you are interested. The M.B.A. program requires a once-a-term visit to the Gainesville campus; the Pharmacy program requires regular in-class work at one of 10 evaluation sites in Florida.

Admissions Information

Academic Disciplines
General business administration, engineering, pharmacy. Within the engineering program are these disciplines: aerospace engineering, mechanics, and engineering science; civil engineering; computer and information sciences and engineering; electrical and computer engineering; industrial and systems engineering; materials science and engineering; mechanical engineering; and nuclear and radiological engineering.

Degrees Offered
M.B.A., M.E., M.S., Pharm.D.

Admissions Requirements
Business—The candidate should have at least two years of full-time professional work experience after college graduation. All

candidates must have taken the GMAT within the last five years, and must submit original transcripts, essay, and letters of recommendation. Everyone must be interviewed either on the telephone or in person. Engineering—An undergraduate degree from an accredited institution; a minimum grade of B for all upper-division undegraduate work; a minimum of 1000 total Verbal-Quantitative score on the GRE. Pharmacy—Candidate must be a graduate of a college of pharmacy with a recognized bachelor's degree and be licensed to practice pharmacy.

Equipment Requirements
Business—IBM-compatible computer featuring a Pentium 166 CPU or better, 32 MB RAM, 1 GB hard drive, CD-ROM drive, 56K modem, sound card with speakers and microphone, and a small personal video camera. The estimated cost of all equipment is $3,000. Engineering—Access to a VHS videotape player or video teleconference equipment with H.320 standards (112/128 Kbps). Pharmacy—IBM-compatible computer featuring a Pentium CPU with Windows 95 operating system, 16 MB RAM, CD-ROM, modem (28.8), and printer.

Tuition and Other Fees
Business—A total of $29,500–$32,000 is estimated for tuition and supplies. Other costs include travel to Gainesville once per term, airfare for one European trip, and the aforementioned computer equipment. Engineering—Same as standard nonresident tuition: $434.40 per credit hour in 1997–98. Pharmacy—$1,825 per semester, plus unspecified additional fees associated with graduate-level study.

Credits Transferable?
Business—Yes. Engineering—Yes. Pharmacy—No.

Program Information

Delivery System
Business—The majority of the content is delivered through asynchronous methods. Individual instructors may hold real-time meetings via the Internet for such activities as review sessions. Teams may also hold real-time chat sessions. Engineering—Primarily through videotape. A few selected courses are delivered

in real time using interactive video teleconferencing equipment. Pharmacy—Online, videotape, and on-site work at one of 10 evaluation sites.

Year Established
Business—The online program will begin in May 1998. The executive M.B.A. program has existed for the past four years. Engineering—1964. Pharmacy—1994.

Number of Courses
Business—16. Engineering—78. Pharmacy—9

Total Number of Faculty
Business—Approximately 20. Engineering—Approximately 75 per year. Pharmacy—25.

Student Demographics
Business—Unknown at this time. Engineering—Primarily adult learners seeking professional development. Pharmacy— Approximately 50 percent institutional and 50 percent community pharmacists. The median age is approximately 35. Most students live within close driving range of 10 evaluation sites in the state.

Dropout Rate
Pharmacy—5 percent. Rates for business and engineering are not available.

Accreditation
Business—American Assembly of Collegiate Schools of Business (AACSB). Engineering—The Engineering Accreditation Commission of the Accreditation Board for Engineering and Technology (ABET) has accredited programs in all departments offering baccalaureate degrees. Pharmacy—American Council on Pharmaceutical Education.

Class Information

Average Class Size
Business—First class will be limited to no more than 40–45 students. Engineering—5. Pharmacy—13.

TAs for Large Classes?
Business—No. Engineering—Varies by department. Pharmacy—Yes.

Length of Session or Semester
Business—Each term is approximately 10 weeks in length. Engineering—Follows the university semester system of two 16-week periods and two 6-week summer terms. Pharmacy—21 hours of taped content and 24 hours of experiential work and evaluation.

Sessions Required for Degree
Business—Seven terms plus an orientation and a European trip. Engineering—Varies, depending on number of courses completed each semester. A complete nonthesis degree program takes three and two-thirds years at the completion rate of one graduate engineering course per semester, including summer sessions. Pharmacy—Varies according to clinical experience.

Time Commitment per Course
Business—Same as all other M.B.A. programs. Engineering—Varies, depending on course requirements and student ability. Pharmacy—120 to 150 hours based on prior clinical knowledge and experience.

Participation Expected
Business—Participation in both class activities and team activities is expected. Engineering—Varies. Pharmacy—Participation required.

Access to Faculty
Business—E-mail or one-to-one desktop videoconferencing. Engineering—E-mail, telephone, fax, mail. Pharmacy—E-mail, telephone, pager.

Grading Procedure
Business—Same as on campus. Engineering—Same as on campus. Pharmacy—Case presentation, homework, written exam, and class participation.

Testing Procedure

Business—During the term, assignments are submitted via Lotus Notes. Students come to Gainesville once per term for exams. Engineering—All exams administered to distance education students must be proctored. Pharmacy—Two open-book exams online plus clinical skills assessment.

Telling Details

Average Class Load per Instructor

Business—Only one distance-learning course in addition to on-campus teaching responsibilities. Engineering—Two courses per semester on average. Pharmacy—No information is available.

Faculty Compensation

Business—Yes. Engineering—No, but distance-learning activities receive consideration in the tenure process. Pharmacy—Yes.

Remote Access to Library

Business and Engineering—Students have dial-in access to library networks through the State University System's Library User Information System (LUIS). Pharmacy—No

Other Library Resources Available or Recommended

Business—All M.B.A. students have access to LEXIS/NEXIS via the Internet for their research needs. Engineering—Yes. Pharmacy—Yes

University of Houston

Address

2700 Bay Area Boulevard
Houston, TX 77058

Phone: (281) 395-2800 or (800) 687-3488
Fax: (281) 395-2639
E-mail: mshopt@bay.6.uh.edu
URL: http://www.uh.edu/academics/de/

Contact Person
Dr. Marshall Shopt

Description

The University of Houston operates an enormous off-campus program. More than 3,000 students are taking satellite courses at corporate, government, academic, and alternative sites, forming their own cohorts. Discussion at each site and participation among the sites via audiobridge are essential parts of the program. Houston has a powerful curriculum development area that assists faculty in the task of turning their curriculum into effective television.

Admissions Information

Academic Disciplines
Engineering, computers, hospitality, and manual training

Degrees Offered
Master's degrees in engineering, industrial engineering, and electrical engineering, and engineering

Admissions Requirements
Varies by department and program. Most include a bachelor's degree (arts or sciences) from an accredited college and GRE or GMAT.

Equipment Requirements

Telvision, computer, modem, and satellite downlink. There are four sites in the Houston area offering computer access.

Tuition and Other Fees

For residents, $390 per three semester hours. For nonresidents, $960 per three semester hours. There is also a $50 fee per semester.

Credits Transferable

Limited. No more than 6–9 credits are transferable.

Program Information

Delivery System

Compressed video, satellite, video, videotape, and the Internet

Year Established

1983

Number of Courses

Approximately 15 per semester

Number of Faculty

35

Student Demographics

Students are young professionals in their late 20s and early 30s with a few years of work experience. Most are from corporations in the Houston area.

Dropout Rate

Currently under study.

Accreditation

Southern Association of Colleges and Schools

Class Information

Average Class Size

15

TAs for Large Classes?
Yes

Length of Session or Semester
16 weeks

Sessions Required for Degree
Typically 36 hours (12 courses)

Time Commitment per Course
About six hours

Participation Expected
Interactivity is required.

Access to Faculty
E-mail and telephone

Grading Procedure
A–F

Testing Procedure
At the discretion of the professor. Some testing is administered on the Internet, some at proctored sites, and some on campus.

Telling Details

Average Class Load per Instructor
Varies. Most faculty take one distance-learning course in addition to their regular class load.

Faculty Compensation
Yes, there is extra compensation.

Remote Access to Library?
Yes

Other Library Resources Available or Recommended
Library sharing, networks, databases, and the World Wide Web

University of Idaho

Address

College of Engineering
Engineering Outreach
Moscow, ID 83844

Phone: (800) 824-2889
Fax: (208) 885-6168
E-mail: outreach@uidaho.edu
URL: http://www.uidaho.edu/evo

Contact Person
Barry Willis, (208) 885-6373
E-mail: bwillis@uidaho.edu

Description

The University of Idaho has carefully planned and expanded its distance offerings. It now has complete degree programs in 12 disciplines and uses many delivery systems. While participating fully in collaborative programs, it is a primary deliverer of educational programs. Each program is offered on a five-year schedule to fit in with the demands of the university. Each is revised for the next cycle, and the appropriate technology utilized. Students may find the same course in different modalities.

Admissions Information

Academic Disciplines
Engineering, biological and agricultural engineering, computer science, computer engineering, electrical engineering, geological engineering, mechanical engineering, metallurgical engineering, mining engineering, human facto psychology, and technical math.

Degrees Offered
Master of Science or Master of Engineering (depends on the student's thesis option) in the above disciplines

Admissions Requirements
Same as on-campus students: A bachelor's degree from an accredited college and any other relevant particulars.

Equipment Requirements
Video player, computer, modem, and Internet access

Tuition and Other Fees
$328 per credit hour

Credits Transferable
To be negotiated

Program Information

Delivery System
Typically videotaped instruction, but also compressed video, satellite, microwave, print, and the Internet

Year Established
Idaho began offering video courses in 1975.

Number of Courses
90–95 per semester

Number of Faculty
Two hundred fifty of the on campus faculty offer some distance learning courses.

Student Demographics
From 400 to 500 professional adult students. Only 30 percent are from Idaho.

Dropout Rate
Ninety-two percent finish each course and 80 percent get their degrees.

Accreditation
Midwest Association of Schools and Colleges

Class Information

Average Class Size
5 in a single site

TAs for Large Classes?
As needed

Length of Session or Semester
5 months

Sessions Required for Degree
Typically, a student takes one class a semester for five years. This varies with the program.

Time Commitment per Course
Not available.

Participation Expected
The student must participate actively in some format.

Access to Faculty
E-mail. There is also a toll-free number for students to call faculty.

Grading Procedure
A–F

Testing Procedure
Proctored tests at the student's site. Students procure their own proctors.

Telling Details

Average Class Load per Instructor
2 courses

Faculty Compensation
Faculty receive $55 per student per credit.

Remote Access to Library?
Yes

Other Library Resources Available or Recommended
Yes

University of Illinois

Address

1206 South Sixth Street
218 Commerce West
Champaign, IL 61820

Phone: (217) 333-4510
Fax   (217) 333-3242
E-mail: tatum@uisuc.edu
URL: http://www.cba.uiuc.edu

Contact Person
Merle Giles

Description

This is a relatively new Executive M.B.A. program aimed primarily at Illinois residents. Students go to the campus or corporate sites for all-day sessions on alternating Fridays and Saturdays. There are four semesters in a program. An international residency is required in which the student works to solve a specific corporate problem. The entire degree program uses the case-study method and is highly individualized for each student.

Admissions Information

Academic Disciplines
Business

Degrees Offered
Executive M.B.A.

Admissions Requirements
A bachelor's degree from an accredited institution, GMAT (if the student has no degree), 7–10 years of work experience (including 5 years in management), interview, and three letters of support.

Equipment Requirements
Computer, modem, corporate site

Tuition and Other Fees
$17,325

Credits Transferable?
Yes

Program Information

Delivery System
Videoconference and real-time classes via computer.

Year Established
1994

Number of Courses
16

Number of Faculty
16

Student Demographics
Midcareer professionals, ages 27 to 51. There is an even ratio of men and women.

Accreditation?
American Assembly of Collegiate Schools of Business

Class Information

Average Class Size
36

TAs for Large Classes?
No

Length of Session or Semester
15 weeks

Sessions Required for Degree
16

Time Commitment per Course
Three to ten hours per class beyond instruction. Some of this time is spent in online study groups.

Participation Expected
Depends upon the instructor; all courses require participation in study groups.

Access to Faculty
Telephone, E-mail

Grading Procedure
A–F

Testing Procedure
Someone is at each site to act as facilitator or proctor.

Telling Details

Average Class Load per Instructor
1

Faculty Compensation
Distance learning is part of the regular teaching load.

Remote Access to Library?
Company libraries are used rather than a university library.

Other Library Resources Available or Recommended
World Wide Web and databases

University of Iowa

Address

Center for Credit Programs
116 International Center
Iowa City, IA 52242-1802

Phone: (800) 272-6430 or (319) 335-2575
Fax: (319) 335-2740
E-mail: credit-programs@uiowa.du
URL: http://www.uiowa.edu/~ccp

Contact Person
Scot Wilcox
Phone: (319)335-2044
E-mail: scot-wilcox@uiowa.edu

Admissions Information

Class Information
Higher education, pharmacy, business administration, social work, computer science, electrical and computer engineering, and science education

Degrees Offered
M.A., M.S., M.S.W., M.B.A., M.S.W.

Admissions Requirements
Access to one of a range of sites within the state of Iowa; bachelor's degree from a regionally accredited school with a GPA of at least 2.3; other requirements vary by program

Equipment Requirements
Internet access is preferred, but typewriter or word processor is sufficient.

Tuition and Other Fees
$221 per semester hour for M.B.A. program. $184 per semester hour for Pharm.D. program. $170 per semester hour for all other programs.

Credits Transferable?
Yes, with some restrictions

Delivery System
Iowa Communications Network (site-based, real-time interactive video); on-site instruction at selected cities within state of Iowa; videotape; occasional correspondence study

Year Established
Graduate off-campus degree programs began were established in the 1970s. New programs have been added intermittently.

Number of Courses
Thirty to sixty semester hours, depending upon the program

Number of Faculty
Approximately 100 across the various programs.

Accreditation
North Central Association of Colleges and Schools. Additional accreditations are program specific.

Class Information

Average Class Size
As low as three for a given site on the Iowa Communications Network, or as many as 30 on site.

TAs for Large Classes?
TAs are not employed for graduate instruction.

Length of Session or Semester
16 weeks, including finals week

Sessions Required for Degree
Varies by program and the number of courses for which a student enrolls each semester.

Time Commitment per Course
Approximately 45 contact hours, plus study time (an additional 90 hours or so)

Participation Expected
Varies by program

Access to Faculty
Course evaluations written by students; standard departmenal procedures

Grading Procedure
Depends on the course instructor

Testing Procedure
Proctored or on-site exams

Telling Details

Average Class Load per Instructor
Typically one distance-learning course in addition to other departmental load

Faculty Compensation
Yes

Remote Access to Library
Limited, though internet technologies should allow for increased access

Other Library Resources Available or Recommended
Yes

University of Maine

Address

Education Network of Maine
46 University Drive
Augusta, ME 04330

Phone: (800) 868-7000
Fax: (207) 621-3062
E-mail: jrusso@enm.maine.edu
URL: http://www.enm.maine.edu

Contact Person
Pam McBrayne
Phone: (207) 621-3333

Description

From its beginnings as a network with sites in the remotest parts of Maine, this program has offered those who live on one of the state's many islands or otherwise far from an institution of higher education the opportunity to learn. The major demographic of the program's early days—women in their 30s who could not matriculate at a nearby college—has persisted, but today the Educational Network of Maine has expanded beyond its original intent. Courses and degree programs come not only from the University of Maine, but from other institutions beyond its borders. The consituency is still residents of Maine, but the delivery systems and the offerings have greatly expanded.

Admissions Information

Academic Disciplines
Liberal studies, education, health, business, public policy, health policy, nursing.

Degrees Offered

M.A. in liberal studies, M.S. in educational leadership, M.S. in health policy and management, M.B.A. from the University of South Carolina, and graduate certificate programs

Admissions Requirements
Varies according to program

Equipment Requirements
Computer and ITV based

Tuition and Other Fees
$167–$179 per credit hour; M.B.A. higher

Credits Transferable?
Sometimes

Program Information

Delivery System
Local cable companies, interactive ITV system designed in 1988. Broadcast by Instructional Television Fixed Service (ITFS) to sites throughout the state of Maine. Additionally they use Internet, videotapes, computer conferencing, and a telephone bridge

Year Established
1989

Student Demographics
The majority of students are over the age of 30. Seventy-four percent are female. With over 100 local sites, most travel about 10 miles to an classroom equipped with instructional television (ITV).

Accreditation
New England Association of Schools and Colleges

Class Information

Average Class Size
Depends on the technology and the program.

TAs for Large Classes?
Yes

Length of Session or Semester
Depends on the program. The average is six to nine semester hours of seminar credit, 15–21 hours of additional graduate credit, and six hours of Master Project credit. For the M.B.A. program—54 credit hours.

Sessions Required for Degree
Programs take 2–3 years to complete.

Time Commitment per Course
Same as if it was on campus.

Participation Expected
Some faculty require live participation, while others give traditional lectures.

Access to Faculty
E-mail, voice mail

Grading Procedure
A–D

Testing Procedure
Students are tested online or at any of 100 sites.

Telling Details

Average Class Load per Instructor
A distance-learning class counts as two on-campus classes.

Faculty Compensation
None.

Remote Access to Library?
URSUS, the University of Maine Libraries, the Maine State Library, Bangor Public Library, Bates and Bowdoin online libraries. There is a unique off-campus library department and a toll-free reference service.

Other Library Resources Available or Recommended
The central office sends out additional materials and has a great many accessible databases.

University of Massachusetts, Amherst

Address

College of Engineering
Video Instructional Program
113 Marcus Hall
Amherst, MA 01003

Phone: (413) 545-0063
Fax: (413) 545-1227
E-mail: vip@vip.ecs.umass.edu
URL: http://zonker.ecs.umass.edu/vip/index.html

Contact Person
Stephen Levey, Director

Description

The long-established program at University of Massachusetts is a hybrid of the Engineering and Continuing Education Departments. In each academic area the course is offered both on campus and via videotape. Each week there are 150 minutes of lecture for a three-credit course. On Fridays the videotapes and all materials are shipped to off-site students, to be received the following Tuesday. The off-campus students receive the same assignments and tests as the students on campus. The courses to be televised each semester take place in a studio classroom.

Admissions Information

Academic Disciplines
Engineering and computer science

Degrees Offered
M.S. and Ph.D. in electrical and computer engineering, M.S. in engineering management, M.S. in computer science

Admissions Requirements
An undergraduate or master's degree from an accredited institution, a 2.75 GPA (master's students only), two letters of recommendation, and GRE. Students from countries where English isn't spoken must take the TOEFL.

Equipment Requirements
VCR, optional computer and modem

Tuition and Other Fees
$1,225 per 3-credit course, $20 registration fee

Credits Transferable?
The university will accept up to six credits from another institution, and will also accept all credits from related NTU courses.

Overall Program Information

Delivery System
Videotape

Year Established
1974

Number of Courses
50

Number of Faculty
47

Student Demographics
Working professionals. There are more males than females. The range of ages is 23–50

Dropout Rate
10 percent

Accreditation
New England Association of Schools and Colleges

Class Information

Average Class Size
15

TAs for Large Classes?
There are teaching assistants for all courses; two if the class is large.

Length of Session or Semester
14 weeks

Sessions Required for Degree
30–36 credits. There are three semesters per year.

Time Commitment per Course
2–3 hours plus the tapes

Participation Expected
A referral list is developed for students to participate among themselves.

Access to Faculty
Phone and E-mail

Grading Procedure
A–F

Testing Procedure
Both proctored and unproctored exams. Sometimes the students find their own proctors.

Telling Details

Average Class Load per Instructor
2 courses

Faculty Compensation
Yes

Remote Access to Library?
Students can reach the UMass Library system through the Internet.

Other Library Resources Available or Recommended
Databases, specific web sites

University of Memphis

Address

Department of Journalism
3711 Veterans Avenue
Memphis TN 38152

Phone: (901) 678-2401
Fax: (901) 678-4287
E-mail: ewbrody@memphis.edu
URL: http://umvirtual.memphis.edu

Description

This master's degree in journalism is geared towards practicing professionals seeking to enhance their career potential.

Admissions Information

Academic Disciplines
Journalism, with emphases in print and electronic journalism, advertising, and public relations.

Degrees Offered
M.A.

Admissions Requirements
3.0 undergraduate GPA. Scores of 70 on Miller, Analogies Test or 900 with 500 on the verbal component of the GRE. Students may take up to three courses as nondegree candidates and petition for exceptions to degree requirements.

Equipment Requirements
IBM-compatible computer with a 486SX CPU or faster (Pentium is recommended), a 14.4 modem (28.8 recommended) with a Winsock-compliant network software product, and a hard drive with at least 6 MB available (12 MB recommended) for program-

related software and user files. Internet access providing a direct TCP/IP connection to the University of Memphis server is necessary. A local Internet access provider is recommended. Students can access the University of Memphis server directly via telephone, but long distance costs can be prohibitive.

Tuition and Other Fees
$1,000 per three-semester hour course, including all texts and materials. Program requirements are 30 to 36 semester hours.

Credits Transferable?
Up to six semester hours

Overall Program Information

Delivery System
Real-time weekly class meetings during evening hours. Days and times set in keeping with mutual convenience of class members.

Year Established
1996

Number of Courses
There are 28 courses available. Students are required to complete a four-course core and then select from remaining courses in keeping with personal objectives.

Number of Faculty
Minimum of four, varying with courses students select.

Student Demographics
Most are 30 to 50 years old, with full-time jobs in journalism.

Dropout Rate
Approximately 15 percent, almost universally due to career changes.

Accreditation
Southern Association of Colleges and Schools, Accrediting Council for Eduation in Journalism and Mass Communication.

Class Information

Average Class Size
6 to 10

TAs for Large Classes?
No

Length of Session or Semester
six weeks

Sessions Required for Degree
10 at minimum

Time Commitment per Course
50 to 60 hours (estimated)

Participation Expected
Students are expected to actively participate in real time online class meetings which require prior reading.

Access to Faculty
Primarily via E-mail. Otherwise in classroom or via telephone.

Grading Procedure
The university assigns whole letter grades on a 4.0 scale.

Testing Procedure
Timed tests are administered electronically. In many courses, research papers are used in lieu of formal testing.

Telling Details

Average Class Load per Instructor
Three courses per 13-week on-campus semester; no more than one online course at a time.

Faculty Compensation
Yes

Remote Access to Library?
Students can access the library via the university computer. The library's Interlibrary Loan Office retrieves, ships, and tracks any materials that students cannot access in electronic form through the library (including 32 online databases).

Other Library Resources Available or Recommended
Access to other libraries can be helpful but is not necessary.

University of Nebraska

Address

Department of Academic Telecommunications
Clifford Hardin Nebraska Center for Continuing Education
P.O. Box 839805
Lincoln NE 68583

Phone: (402) 472-0400
Fax: (402) 472-4345
E-mail: atc@unlinfo.unl.edu
URL: http://www.unl.edu

Contact Person
Bea Gatliff
E-mail: bgatliff@unlinfo.unl.edu

Description

This is a fine satellite and Internet program. Unfortunately for the rest of us, it is confined to the residents of Nebraska. The school is known for the development of excellent video even when the topics are less than interesting. Many corporations and academic institutions take advantage of the university's offerings, achieving Master's degrees without having to travel to the campus. It is a valuable opportunity for those in the area.

Admissions Information

Academic Disciplines
Engineering and journalism

Degrees Offered
Master's degrees in systems engineering, industrial and management systems engineering, computer science, and journalism

Admissions Requirements
Varies according to program. A bachelor's degree from an accredited institution and a background in engineering or science are generally required.

Equipment Requirements
Public and corporate sites must have computer access and an audiobridge for interactive or videoconferencing. Students need a computer, a modem, and an Internet access provider.

Tuition and Other Fees
$622.50 per three-credit course in engineering

$467.25 per three-credit course in journalism

Credits Transferable
Considered by department

Program Information

Delivery System
Satellite (real time) mixed with Internet (asynchronous) delivery.

Year Established
Engineering—1986, Journalism—1991

Number of Courses
About 15 per semester

Number of Faculty
15–20 per semester

Student Demographics
Residents of Nebraska between the ages of 35–50. Engineering students are mostly male, and journalism students are mostly female.

Dropout Rate
Not available

Accreditation
North Central Association of Schools and Colleges

Class Information

Average Class Size
10

TAs for Large Classes?
Unnecessary because classes are small.

Length of Session or Semester
15 weeks

Sessions Required for Degree
Varies with the degree

Time Commitment per Course
Same as on-campus students

Participation Expected
Little participation in engineering program, but heavy participation in journalism

Access to Faculty
Telephone and E-mail

Grading Procedure
4-point system

Testing Procedure
Proctored exams at public and corporate sites

Telling Details

Average Class Load per Instructor
Depends on the department

Faculty Compensation
Sometimes

Remote Access to Library?
Yes

Other Library Resources Available or Recommended
Individual students discover their own resources.

University of New England

Address

Hills Beach Road
Biddeford, ME 04005

Phone: (207) 283-0171
Fax: (207) 282-6379
E-mail: cpes@mailbox.une.edu
URL: http://www.une.edu

Contact Person
John Brant

Description

The University of New England recently merged with Westbrook College. The two sites are moving together. More than $2 million has been spent on new technology, including videoconferencing, new computer labs, studios, and classrooms. The distance learning program uses prerecorded tapes in conjunction with text. Students at local sites work in teams. The program is delivered to teachers and administrators working at school sites.

Admissions Information

Academic Disciplines
Education

Degrees Offered
Master's degree in education

Admissions Requirements
Certification as a teacher, access to a classroom of students, transcripts, and a personal statement.

Equipment Requirements
A television and a VCR

Tuition and Other Fees
$235 per credit hour (most courses are three credits), $60 materials fee, and general fees

Credits Transferable
Up to 6

Program Information

Delivery System
Videotape and E-mail

Year Established
1995

Number of Courses
11

Number of Faculty
3 full-time, 12 adjunct

Student Demographics
Teachers and a range of professionals who want education for self-improvement. The teachers range from preschool to postsecondary with an average work experience of between 10 and 15 years.

Dropout Rate
Roughly 24 out of 400 so far

Accreditation
New England Association of Schools and Colleges

Class Information

Average Class Size
35

TAs for Large Classes?
No. Additional sections are added

Length of Session or Semester
16 weeks. The summer session is 12 weeks.

Sessions Required for Degree
33 credits

Time Commitment per Course
5 hours per week

Participation Expected
All group activities are held on site

Access to Faculty
E-mail, phone, and fax

Grading Procedure
A–F

Testing Procedure
All tests consist of open essays. There is also one collaborative research project.

Telling Details

Average Class Load per Instructor
7 courses (or sections) per year

Faculty Compensation
Full-time faculty are paid the same on campus or at a distance. Adjuncts are paid per enrollee.

Remote Access to Library?
Students can receive materials by contacting the office. The Interlibrary Loan system is also used.

Other Library Resources Available or Recommended
Resources on Web sites

University of Notre Dame

Address

Executive Programs
Suite 126, College of Business Administration
P. O. Box 399
Notre Dame, Indiana 46556-0399

Phone: (219) 631-3622
Fax: (219) 631-9483
E-mail: arnoldfludwig1@nd.edu
URL: http://www.nd.edu/-execprog

Contact Person
Arnold Ludwig, Assistant Dean of Executive Education

Description

This Executive M.B.A., delivered on-site to large corporations, is an extension of a traditional M.B.A. program with more attention paid to real-life issues of working managers. Intense discussion occurs around human and policy questions. There is a logical sequence of courses leading to the degree; however, the special needs and the background of strategies available to the experienced manager are recognized and used as building blocks for planning. The program merges functional, quantitative-analytical, and qualitative-behavioral management paradigms, and utilizes some of the latest technology tools, including two-way videoconferencing. There are now three distance classrooms: Owens-Illinois world headquarters in Toledo, Ohio; the Carrier Corporation in Indianapolis, Indiana; and Ameritech Headquarters in Hoffman, Illinois.

Admissions Information

Academic Disciplines
Business and management

Degrees Offered
Executive M.B.A.

Admissions Requirements
An undergraduate degree (or GMAT for those without one), at least five years of meaningful management experience, demonstrated motivation, approval of employer, and the ability to use Excel, Word, Power Point, and E-mail (2-day teaching workshops on campus)

Equipment Requirements
Three fully-equipped distance learning classrooms developed and maintained by the university. A home computer and modem are suggested.

Tuition and Other Fees
$23,690 for the 1997–98 academic year, $2,000 nonrefundable confirmation fee

Credits Transferable?
Yes, from another executive M.B.A. program

Overall Program Information

Delivery System
2-way compressed video, fully interactive two-way audio in two remote classrooms

Year Established
1995

Number of Courses
16. There are no electives.

Number of Faculty
16

Student Demographics
The mean age is 35. All participants are middle managers, of which 25 percent are female and seven percent are minorities. About 50 percent come from the manufacturing field.

Dropout Rate
One student has dropped out.

Accreditation
American Assembly of Collegiate Schools of Business.

Class Information

Average Class Size
56

TAs for Large Classes?
No; every four to six students are in a study group with a resident expert; study groups meet for four hours each week

Length of Session or Semester
15 week semesters

Sessions Required for Degree
16 courses

Time Commitment per Course
40 hours per week (very intense)

Participation Expected
Strong participation is required from each student.

Access to Faculty
E-mail

Grading Procedure
Conventional A–F grading is used. Students must maintain a cumulative average of 3.0 in order to graduate.

Testing Procedure
There is a resident facilitator at each site for testing. Students must reside on campus for six days at the start of the program.

Telling Details

Average Class Load per Instructor
2 courses

Faculty Compensation
Yes; faculty demonstrate a strong commitment night and day and
receive extra compensation for teaching in the program

Remote Access to Library?
Yes, through both America Online and the university

Other Library Resources Available or Recommended
No

University of Phoenix

Address

Online Campus
100 Spear Street
San Francisco, CA 94105

Phone: (415) 541-0141
Fax: (415) 541-0761
E-mail: (through web site)
URL: http://www.uophx.edu

Contact Person
Terry Hedegaard

Description

The University of Phoenix program is in many ways a model for online education. The faculty are selected not only for their subject matter expertise, but their ability to conduct classes through the computer. They are trained and mentored throughout their time with the programs. All students must participate five days a week, initiating a routine that serves them well in the continuity of each course. Cluster groups are kept small so that students know each other and collaborate in each other's learning. There is a low dropout rate and a high success ratio. Students have great words of praise for both the faculty and their own learning.

Admissions Information

Academic Disciplines
Business, computers

Degrees Offered
M.A. in organizational management, M.B.A., M.B.A. in technology management, M.B.A. in global management, M.S. in computer information systems

Admissions Requirements
Bachelor's degree from a regionally accredited institution, three years of work with exposure to organizational systems. Students from countries where English isn't spoken must take the TOEFL.

Equipment Requirements
DOS, Windows 3.1 or Windows 95; Recommended 486 CPU or faster with 12 MB RAM, 28.8 modem, and proprietary software (AlexWare)

Tuition and Other Fees
$425 per credit hour

Credits Transferable?
Yes

Overall Program Information

Delivery System
All programs are online using Alex, the proprietary system

Year Established
1989

Number of Courses
70 courses

Number of Faculty
70 at any one time out of 248 active faculty

Student Demographics
Typically, they are midcareer professionals. The average age is 38. Seventy-two percent are males, with increasing numbers of females each year. Many students travel frequently, making online learning most convenient. Most are Americans, some living internationally.

Dropout Rate
5–7 percent

Accreditation
Commission on Institutions of Higher Education of North Central Association of Colleges and Schools.

Class Information

Average Class Size
8–13

Length of Session or Semester
Online classes 5–6 weeks in length

Sessions Required for Degree
Most students complete degree in two-and-a-half to three years

Time Commitment per Course
15–20 hours per week

Participation Expected
Student must come online five days per week to participate in class discussions. This intense, frequent communication keeps the dropout rate low.

Access to Faculty
Online

Grading Procedure
Work is graded in a narrative fashion.

Testing Procedure
Students undergo both cognitive and affective assessment before and after program.

Telling Details

Average Class Load per Instructor
One class

Faculty Compensation
Two full-time faculty work with program. All others are adjunct faculty, working online.

Remote Access to Library?
Learning Resource Center On-Line Library, additional databases,
and Selected Internet Links

Other Library Resources Available or Recommended
No

University of South Carolina

Address

Department of Physics and Astronomy
Columbia, SC 29208

Phone: (803) 777-6466
Fax: (803) 777-3065
E-mail: safko@sc.edu
URL: http://astro.physics.sc.edu

Contact Person
John L. Safko

Description

Selected courses to aid teachers or MAT or MT students with material in physics and astronomy. Four courses are offered. PHYS J781—Astronomy for Teachers; PHYS J787—String and Sticky Tape Demonstrations, SMED J541/542—General physics for teachers.

Admissions Information

Academic Disciplines
Physics and astronomy

Degrees Offered
None. The courses named above are graduate-level and often used as part of recertification.

Admissions Requirements
A student may be admitted as a special student or as a degree-seeking student in another program (usually education).

Equipment Requirements
Provided or easily obtained locally

Credits Transferable?
Yes

Program Information

Delivery System
Videocassette. Real-time delivery is used only for exams.

Year Established
1977

Number of Courses
4

Number of Faculty
2

Student Demographics
Primarily nontraditional students; mostly teachers and teacher prep students throughout the world

Dropout Rate
Low

Accreditation
Southern Association for Colleges and Schools

Class Information

Average Class Size
Less than 20

TAs for Large Classes?
No

Length of Session or Semester
15 weeks

Time Commitment per Course
Varies

Participation Expected
Little: Courses are watched on videocassette. Two courses do have at least one on-campus meeting scheduled.

Access to Faculty
Letters, phone, and E-mail

Grading Procedure
Written homework and exams

Testing Procedure
Proctored exams at distance sites or (for PHYS 787) take-home exams

Telling Details

Average Class Load per Instructor
1–2

Faculty Compensation
Faculty receives extra pay for teaching-distance learning.

Remote Access to Library?
Yes

Other Library Resources Available or Recommended
Yes

University of Tennessee

Address

Business Administration Program
University of Tennessee, Chattanooga
Siskin Building
615 McCallie Avenue
Chattanooga, TN 37421

Phone: (423) 755-4210
Fax: (423) 755-5255
E-mail: ashley-williams@utc.edu

Contact Person
Ashley Williams

Criminal Justice Program
University of Tennessee, Chattanooga
109 Health and Human Services
615 McCallie Avenue
Chattanooga, TN 37403

Phone: (423) 755-4135
Fax: (423) 755-4132
E-mail   karen-casey@utc.edu

Contact Person
Dr. Karen Casey

Nursing
University of Tennessee, Memphis
College of Nursing
877 Madison Avenue
Memphis, TN 38163

Phone: (901) 448-7464
Fax: (901) 448-4121
E-mail: ptagg@utmem1.utmem.edu

Contact Person
Dr. Peggy Tagg Veeser

Description

This land-grant institution offers a number of different graduate degree programs, originating from campuses in Memphis and Chattanooga, as well as from its main Knoxville campus. These are all interactive video courses, and require students to be within driving distance of the distance learning sites at which the courses are shown.

Admissions Information

Academic Disciplines
Business Administration, Criminal Justice, Nursing

Degrees Offered
Business Administration—MBA; Criminal Justice—M.S.; Nursing—M.S.N., Ph.D.

Admissions Requirements
Business—Admission to the university's Chattanooga Graduate Division, GPA of at least 2.5. Students must also score a 950 in an index where the student's GPA is multiplied by 200 and added to the student's GMAT score. Criminal Justice—A bachelor's degree from an accredited college, minimum GPA of 2.5, official score for the MAT or GRE, supplemental data form, brief essay, and two letters of recommendation. Nursing—A degree in nursing from an institution accredited by the National League for Nursing.

Equipment Requirements
Business—none. Criminal Justice—none. Nursing—access to a computer.

Tuition and Other Fees
Business and Criminal Justice—$151 per credit for in-state students; $351 per credit for out-of-state students. Nursing—Approximately $215 per credit hour for in-state students; $530 per credit hour for out-of-state students.

Credits Transferable?
Business and Criminal Justice—A maximum of six semester hours may be transfered into a student's master's program from work taken at an accredited institution. Nursing—Yes.

Program Information

Delivery System
Interactive video (real time). There is also on-site instruction in the business program.

Year Established
Business and Criminal Justice—1993. Nursing—1990

Total Number of Courses
Business—5 plus one on site. Criminal Justice—3. Nursing—10.

Number of Faculty
Business and Criminal Justice—Varies by semester. Nursing—15

Student Demographics
Business and Criminal Justice—Primarily working adults taking courses in the evening. Nursing—Practicing nurses with at least a BSN.

Accreditation
Business—American Assembly of Collegiate Schools of Business. Criminal Justice—Southern Association of Colleges and Schools. Nursing—National League for Nursing

Class Information

Average Class Size
Business—25. Criminal Justice—18. Nursing—35

TAs for Large Classes?
No

Length of Session or Semester
Business and Criminal Justice—15 weeks per semester. Nursing—16 weeks

Sessions Required for Degree
Business—31 credit hours total. Criminal Justice—36 credit hours total. Nursing—3 sessions

Time Commitment per Course
Business and Criminal Justice—45 hours (classes are one evening per week). Nursing—Varies

Participation Expected
Business and Criminal Justice—Varies by instructor. Nursing—100 percent participation required

Access to Faculty
Business and Criminal Justice—E-mail, toll-free telephone, remote site visits by faculty. Nursing—E-mail, toll-free telephone, private interactive video sessions, written correspondence, campus visits by student, and remote site visits by faculty.

Grading Procedure
Varies by instructor

Testing Procedure
Business—Exams (essay and multiple-choice), presentations (group and individual), semester-long projects. Criminal Justice—Exams, presentations, projects, group work. Nursing—Varies by instructor

Telling Details

Average Class Load per Instructor
Business and Criminal Justice—3. Nursing—1 to 2.

Faculty Compensation
Business and Criminal Justice—Not usually. Nursing—No

Remote Access to Library
Business and Criminal Justice—Access to the library at the university's Knoxville branch with a valid University of Tennessee, Chattanooga ID; or access to the Chattanooga branch's library via the World Wide Web.

Other Library Resources Available or Recommended
No

University of Texas at Tyler

Address

3900 University Boulevard
Tyler, TX 75799

Phone: (903) 566-7000
Fax: (903) 566-7127
E-mail: kstewart@mail.uttyl.edu
URL: http://www.uttyl.edu

Contact Person
Dr. Linda Klotz
Phone: (903) 566-7320

Description

Recognizing its geographic isolation and medically underserved community, the University of Texas at Tyler has embarked upon partnerships with other institutions, using technology to deliver high-quality nursing programs. The ongoing M.S. in Nursing–Family Nurse Practitioner program with Texas Tech University has been extremely successful in combining resources, using videoconferencing as an integral part of the instruction and communications system. Every member of the faculty uses the technology for teaching. The university is now embarking upon several strands: Acute Care Nursing, Adult Nurse Practitioner (serving people over 15), and Pediatric and School Nurse Practitioners. All of these will be master's programs with the University of Texas at Arlington.

Admissions Information

Academic Disciplines
Nursing

Degrees Offered
M.S. in Nursing–Family Nurse Practitioner

Admissions Requirements
Bachelor's degree

Equipment Requirements
Telephone, two-way compressed video teaching podiums at either end, computer, modem, and fax machine.

Tuition and Other Fees
Texas residents—$698 for nine semester hours. Non-Texas residents—$2,624 for nine semester hours. Residents of Oklahoma, Arkansas, and Louisiana receive the in-state tuition rate for Texas.

Credits Transferable?
Since two universities share the courses for this program, either school will accept six credits from outside their universities and up to 50 percent of the total credits from the partner school.

Program Information

Delivery System
Two-way compressed video, videotape, audiotape, computer, in person delivery

Year Established
1991 began distance learning
1995 established partnership program

Number of Courses
Over 14

Number of Faculty
31

Student Demographics
Some students come directly from college. A significant percentage are nursing undergraduates who need certification, but most students have about 10 years of experience and want the degree for advancement purposes. About 10 percent of the population is male.

Dropout Rate

The program is still too new to determine this. There were no dropouts in the first class, and two students in the latest group have decided to postpone their studies.

Accreditation

National League for Nursing and the Southern Association for Colleges and Schools

Class Information

Average Class Size
10

TAs for Large Classes?
No. However, each institution has a health clinic attached to the program, and clinic staff are used to assist the students.

Length of Session or Semester
15 weeks, plus a mandatory six to eight week summer program

Sessions Required for Degree
48 semester hours

Time Commitment per Course
In lecture courses, an even ratio of class time to study time is expected. In clinical courses, three hours of study are necessary for each hour at the clinic.

Participation Expected
A high degree of participation is expected. Student meetings and faculty meetings are held on compressed video in addition to classes. Teachers must learn a new way to teach and be aware of the group dynamics when teaching at a distance.

Access to Faculty
Interactive video office hours, computer, fax, and in-person meetings when faculty pay monthly visits.

Grading Procedure
A–F

Testing Procedure
On-site, courier service

Telling Details

Average Class Load per Instructor
Nine to twelve hours, however one hour lecturing is regarded as one clock hour, while one clinical class could be up to nine hours.

Faculty Compensation
The addition of a team teacher and a bonus of $500 for each distance-learning course

Remote Access to Library?
Hospitals and schools must all have libraries. The collections have been increased to accommodate the program. Access is also through computer databases.

Other Library Resources Available or Recommended
A courier service is used between the sites. There is also mailing and faxing of necessary materials.

University of Virginia

Address

School of Engineering Sciences
McCormick Road
Charlottesville, VA 22903

Phone: (804) 924-4057
Fax: (804) 924 4086
E-mail: rfk2u@virginia.edu
URL: http://watt.seas.virginia.edu/~rfk2u/index.html

Contact Person
George Cahen

Description

Several colleges in Virginia have been working together for a number of years to offer engineering courses to each other via a satellite network. They also work with area corporations to upgrade the skills of working professionals who cannot attend on campus. While the classes are delivered by satellite, many classes are videotaped and used at more convenient times. Graduates specialize in one of six subengineering specialties.

Admissions Information

Academic Disciplines
Engineering

Degrees Offered
Master of Engineering in chemical engineering, civil engineering, structural engineering, electrical engineering, material science engineering, mechanical engineering, aerospace engineering, and systems engineering

Admissions Requirements
Undergraduate degree from an accredited institution (at least 60 hours) in a hard science, GPA of 3.0, GRE

Equipment Requirements
An adequate site at a company, government lab, or regional college; a satellite downlink; and an audiobridge. The courses may soon be using streaming video over the Internet.

Tuition and Other Fees
$711 per 3-credit course for Virginia residents, $1,278 for nonresidents

Credits Transferable
Up to 15 credits

Program Information

Delivery System
Satellite, audiobridge, compressed video, and the Internet

Year Established
1983

Number of Courses
8 per semester

Number of Faculty
100

Student Demographics
Young to midlevel professionals. The average student is about five years out of school. The average age 28. Most students are male.

Dropout Rate
Difficult to determine. Some people take the courses for continuing education. Full-degree students leave mainly because they move away or change jobs.

Accreditation
Southern Association of Schools and Colleges

Class Information

Average Class Size
55

TAs for Large Classes?
Teaching assistants are in every class.

Length of Session or Semester
14 weeks and an exam week

Sessions Required for Degree
30 credits

Time Commitment per Course
Significant time. This is a rigorous program. No one should take more than one course per semester.

Participation Expected
Activity is expected through the audiobridge and on the Internet.

Access to Faculty
E-mail and office hours for telephone calls

Grading Procedure
A–F

Testing Procedure
Different strategies are used to administer tests remotely.

Telling Details

Average Class Load per Instructor
1 television course

Faculty Compensation
All full-time faculty receive extra compensation for distance-learning courses given beyond their course load.

Remote Access to Library?
Yes

Other Library Resources Available or Recommended
There are Web sites for each course and regional libraries at certain sites. Others have built up reference collections in nonacademic sites.

University of Waterloo

Address

MOT@Distance
Department of Management Sciences
Faculty of Engineering
University of Waterloo
200 University Avenue West
Waterloo, Ontario Canada N2L 3 G1

Phone: (519) 888-4799
Fax: (519) 746-7252
E-mail: mot@iir.uwaterloo.ca
URL: http://innovate.uwaterloo.ca/mot-de/start.html

Contact Person
Professor Paul D. Guild, Director, Institute for Innovation Research
Phone: (519) 888-4802
E-mail: guild@iir.uwaterloo.ca
URL: http://innovate.uwaterloo.ca/PaulGuild.html

Description

The Management of Technology program option is intended for engineers and scientists who need to deal with technology management in their jobs. Study is undertaken on a part-time basis through the Internet. Students register from across Canada and the United States. The Management of Technology specialization appeals to people who find the "earn as you learn, anywhere, anytime" feature convenient. It adapts proven course materials developed by The Open University (UK). Management of Technology can be defined as: the planning, development, and implementation of technological capabilities for the purpose of attaining the strategic and operational goals of organizations. This area of study addresses both theoretical and empirical underpinnings of the strategies and tools needed for individuals, work groups, and organizations in dealing with the increasing competitive pressures in our global environment. Students complete their degrees with

a final master's project: A personalized, in-depth study of a complex problem, issue, or opportunity in the subject area.

Admissions Information

Academic Discipline
Management sciences, speciality in management of technology

Degrees Offered
Master of Applied Science (MASc)

Admissions Requirements
Applicants should have an honours degree and an excellent academic record from a recognized university. For a MASc, applicants must normally have at least a 75 percent (B) overall standing. Additional requirement information includes three letters of reference, complete transcripts of all previous university studies, and a statement of purpose by the applicant should address the issues of why the candidate wishes to study management sciences, why the candidate will become a future leader in the field, and what unique talents or aptitudes the applicant brings to the profession. Students who do not satisfy all of the admission standards but nonetheless provide evidence of ability to work at a graduate level may be admitted with probationary status.

Equipment Requirements
PC or Mac, 14.4 modem or faster, telephone, TCP/IP service access, some specialized applications which are downloaded without additional cost.

Tuition and Other Fees
$2,500 Canadian per study term (courses last for two terms) or $25,000 Canadian for the degree. Many employers pay the cost of tuition fees in full or in part.

Credits Transferable?
Yes. This is decided on a case-by-case basis.

Program Information

Delivery System

The program includes optional tutorials using the telephone and distance-education technologies of the Internet. Real-time communication is possible but not required. A choice of pacing is also possible by using archived multimedia tutorials when needed. Specific technologies in this program include: Internet access for TCP/IP services, dial-up telephone links or RealAudio over the Internet for shared "audio space," client-server World Wide Web technology for shared "work space," video over the Internet using minicameras for "social space," a computer-managed curriculum archive, and assignments employing search engines and other remote sources. Real time is possible but not required; learner pacing is also possible through the use of archived multimedia tutorials. Course materials (written course notes, texts, audio and video tapes, computer disks) are reproduced and distributed by the university's Distance Education Office. All materials, including the readings of journal articles, are provided in the course materials packages.

Year Established

The full degree program was established in 1997. Individual courses have been delivered this way since 1991.

Number of Courses

6 (each course lasts 2 terms)

Total Number of Faculty

5

Student Demographics

This program is intended for engineers and scientists who need to deal with technology management in their jobs. Students completing studies in the MOT area are prepared for positions in the management of research and design, engineering and development, product design groups, and management consulting.

Accreditation

Ontario Council on Graduate Studies

Class Information

Average Class Size
15 to 29

TAs for Large Classes?
No

Length of Session or Semester
14 weeks per term. Courses last for two terms.

Sessions Required for Degree
10 (5 two-term courses)

Time Commitment per Course
7 to 12 hours per week (part-time study; most students are employed)

Participation Expected
Students read a lot, participate in Internet-based tutorials (including a chat application for submitting questions or comments), interact with instructors via E-mail or telephone, and complete assignments and examinations.

Access to Faculty
Telephone, E-mail, and World Wide Web

Grading Procedure
Rigorous, centrally managed, and evaluated continuously

Testing Procedure
Partly through proctored exams and partly through assignments or projects.

Telling Details

Average Class Load per Instructor
Maximum of two in distance mode; normally four

Faculty Compensation
There is a small inducement and relief from other course duties

Remote Access to Library
Yes, at http://www.lib.uwaterloo.ca/index.html

Other Library Resources Available
World Wide Web

Virginia Polytechnic Institute and State University

Address

Pamplin College of Business
Blacksburg, VA 24061

Phone:	(540) 231-2313
Fax:	(540) 231-3031
E-mail:	mmcphrsn@vt.edu
URL:	http://www.rgs.vt.edu

Contact Person
Dr. Malcolm McPherson, Associate Dean of Research and Graduate Studies

Description

The university uses a satellite system to produce and receive engineering and business courses. The faculty enthusiastically embraces distance learning as a way of offering a broad spectrum of courses to corporate and institutional sites. The interaction of diverse students brings excitement to the master's programs. Recently there was a conversion to digital technology, which should lower the costs of the uplinking activities.

Admissions Information

Academic Disciplines
Business, engineering

Degrees Offered
M.B.A., Master's degrees in engineering, engineering business, civil engineering, mechanical engineering, electrical engineering, industrial and systems engineering

Admissions Requirements
Undergraduate degree from an accredited institution

Equipment Requirements
Satellite downlink, computer, and modem

Tuition and Other Fees
Consult the program's Web page for an updated list of fees.

Credits Transferable
Yes, up to 50 percent of courses from participating schools are transferrable.

Program Information

Delivery System
Satellite and audiobridge (real time)

Year Established
1983

Number of Courses
16

Number of Faculty
50

Student Demographics
Usually people just starting in companies take these courses at a distance. Most students are paid by their company to attend. The age range is 25–35.

Dropout Rate
No different from the university dropout rate.

Accreditation
Southern Association of Colleges and Schools

Class Information

Average Class Size
20

TAs for Large Classes?
Sometimes

Length of Session or Semester
15 weeks

Sessions Required for Degree
30–36 credits

Time Commitment per Course
Very rigorous

Participation Expected
High participation via audiobridge

Access to Faculty
Telephone and E-mail

Grading Procedure
A–F

Testing Procedure
A variety of procedures are used.

Telling Details

Average Class Load per Instructor
2 courses

Faculty Compensation
Faculty receive a few extra perquisites

Remote Access to Library?
Online access

Other Library Resources Available or Recommended
World Wide Web

Walden University

Address

Office of Academic Affairs
155 Fifth Avenue South
Minneapolis, MN 55401

Phone: (800) 444-6795
Fax: (612) 338-5092
E-mail: request@walden.edu
URL: http://www.walden.edu

Contact Person
Christa Scott
Phone: (800) 444-6795, ext. 129

Description

Walden University has developed a unique program designed for changing times in higher education. It is trying to shape a global community of scholars by recognizing the pressures of the workplace and the individual problems of professionals seeking to learn. The university has created a series of doctoral programs that are comprised of a group of seven modules (each requiring a research paper of approximately 100 pages) and a dissertation, all with applications to the modern workplace. The programs can be tailored to the individual's own particular needs. Students from around the world participate in this most innovative and flexible of programs.

Admissions Information

Academic Disciplines
Education, management, health, and human services

Degrees Offered

Master of Science degree in educational change and technology innovation; doctorate degrees in health services, human services, applied management and decision sciences, education, and psychology

Admissions Requirements

Undergraduate or master's degree from an accredited university and a transcript of the student's background. The master's degree requires three years of related work experience.

The degree in operations research requires GRE. Students from countries where English isn't spoken must take the TOEFL.

Equipment Requirements

Computer, 28.8 modem, Internet service provider, and a printer

Tuition and Other Fees

$3,040 per quarter for Knowledge Area Modules, $495 commencement fee, $750 dissertation fee. Master's students must pay $220 per credit, $60 quarterly technology fee, and $495 graduation fee. Psychology students must pay $285 per credit hour (each course is five credits).

Credits Transferable

Only the psychology program allows up to 20 credits in doctoral program. Master's degree will accept up to six hours

Program Information

Delivery System

Online (WIN) network, telecommunications network

Year Established

1970

Number of Courses

50

Number of Faculty

120

Student Demographics
Busy professionals. There is a roughly equal balance of men and women. One third of the students are minorities.

Dropout Rate
45 percent; after six months the rate of those enrolled drops to 10–20 percent

Accreditation
North Central Association of Schools and Colleges

Class Information

Average Class Size
There are no classes, since the program uses one-on-one tutorials. There is one faculty per nine students.

TAs for Large Classes?
Not applicable

Length of Session or Semester
Quarterly (every three months)

Sessions Required for Degree
128 quarter credits. Most programs take three years at one course per quarter. Psychology usually takes four to four-and-a-half years.

Time Commitment per Course
10 hours per week

Participation Expected
A student is required to be in touch with the faculty mentor at least two times per week electronically.

Access to Faculty
E-mail, telephone, fax

Grading Procedure
Satisfactory/Unsatisfactory

Testing Procedure
The approach is very flexible, with projects, research papers, and an oral presentation. The defense of each student's dissertation is conducted by conference call.

Telling Details

Average Class Load per Instructor
Not applicable as there are no classes.

Faculty Compensation
Six full-time department heads—all others are adjunct faculty hired to participate in distance-learning programs.

Remote Access to Library?
Research library at Indiana University

Other Library Resources Available or Recommended
Mailing lists, WIN, listserves, Gopher

Western Michigan University

Address

Division of Continuing Education
Department of Distance Education
Kalamazoo MI 49008

Phone: (616) 387-4216
Fax: (616) 387-4226
E-mail: gail.fredericks@wmich.edu
URL: http://www.wmich.edu

Contact Person
Gail Fredericks

Description

Western Michigan offers a full-fledged M.B.A. program to students nationwide who typically have careers or other responsibilities that would keep them from enrolling in a traditional program. The program combines distance-learning technologies, including compressed video, Web-based instruction, and videotape delay. In addition, the university offers a variety of graduate-level courses via distance learning that vary from semester to semester. Contact the school for more information. The information below applies to the M.B.A. program only.

Admissions Information

Academic Disciplines
Business

Degrees Offered
M.B.A.

Equipment Requirements
Access to a computer is preferred but not necessary.

Tuition and Other Fees
Varies

Credits Transferable?
Some, depending upon the circumstances.

Program Information

Delivery System
Compressed video (real-time) and videotape.

Year Established
1992

Number of Courses
Varies

Number of Faculty
Varies

Student Demographics
27–45 years old; full-time employees in midcareer; typically upwardly mobile with family responsibilities

Dropout Rate
Varies

Accreditation
Western Michigan is accredited by the North Central Association of Schools and Colleges. This program is accredited by the American Assembly of Collegiate Schools of Business.

Class Information

Average Class Size
10–15 students

TAs for Large Classes?
If requested by professor

Length of Session or Semester
13 weeks

Sessions Required for Degree
13

Time Commitment per Course
Varies by course

Participation Expected
Varies by instructor

Access to Faculty
Phone, fax, E-mail

Grading Procedure
Varies by instructor

Testing Procedure
Varies by instructor

Telling Details

Average Class Load per Instructor
Varies

Faculty Compensation
Faculty receive a development fee but no formal tenure credit

Remote Access to Library
Yes

Other Library Resources Available
Computer labs and resource libraries for viewing tapes

Worcester Polytechnic Institute

Address

100 Institute Road
Worcester, MA 01609

Phone: (508) 831-5810
Fax: (508) 831-5881
E-mail: adln@wpi.edu
URL: http://www.wpi.edu/Academics/ADLN

Contact Person
Pennie S. Turgeon
Phone: (508) 831-5810
E-mail: pennie@wpi.edu

Description

In 1979, WPI's commitment to lifelong learning prompted the creation of the Advanced Distance Learning Network (ADLN), a partnership between several academic departments and WPI's Instructional Media Center. Through a combination of information technologies, ADLN makes select WPI courses and programs available to working professionals at their home or place of employment.

Admissions Information

Academic Disciplines
Management and Fire Protection Engineering

Degrees Offered
M.B.A., M.S. in engineering and numerous graduate certificate options

Admissions Requirements
Applicants must hold a B.S. degree in an appropriate field and meet department specific admission standards. All departments require standard forms, official transcripts, and a $50 application fee. Management requires submission of GMAT scores and all international students must submit TOEFL scores.

Equipment Requirements
The minimum requirements are a TV and VCR, a computer with E-mail and World Wide Web access, telephone, and fax. Those wishing to participate via videoconferencing technology must also have access to similar equipment at their place of employment.

Tuition and Other Fees
Tuition is $612 per credit ($1,836 per 3-credit course) for all courses in the 1997–1998 academic year.

Credits Transferable?
Yes

Program Information

Delivery System
Videoconferencing, videotape, World Wide Web, and E-mail

Year Established
Management—1979. Fire protection engineering—1993

Number of Courses
16–20 per year

Number of Faculty
28

Student Demographics
Working professionals across the continental United States, Canada, and England

Dropout Rate
5 percent

Accreditation Agency
New England Association of School and Colleges (WPI overall) and the Accreditation Board for Engineering and Technology (certain academic departments)

Class Information

Average Class Size
12–15

TAs for Large Classes?
Rarely

Length of Session or Semester
14 weeks

Sessions Required for Degree
The 49-credit M.B.A. allows 18 foundation-level credits to be waived for those with appropriate past course work. A 33-credit, nonthesis option is available to those students wishing to pursue a M.S. in fire protection engineering.

Time Commitment per Course
10–12 hours per week in addition to actual class time

Participation Expectation
Class participation requirements vary from course to course.

Access to Faculty
E-mail, phone, fax, and office hours

Grading Procedure
A–F

Testing Procedure
Depending on the course, exams may be electronic, take-home, or proctored. There are also projects and/or research papers.

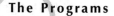

Telling Details

Average Class Load per Instructor
3–5 courses per year depending on course and enrollment levels

Faculty Compensation
Additional compensation in the form of professional development funds.

Remote Access to Library?
Limited to certain collections and online resources

Other Library Resources Available or Recommended
Online databases

Part Three

The Indices

Index by Academic Discipline

Accounting—Empire State College (SUNY)
Advertising—University of Alabama, University of Memphis
Aeronautical science—Embry-Riddle Aeronautical University
Agriculture—Athabasca University, Oklahoma State University
Architecture—Massachusetts Institute of Technology
       Organization Development—Fielding Institute
Behavioral science—California State University—Dominguez Hills
Biology
       Molecular biology—Lehigh University
Business—University of Phoenix, Virginia Polytechnic Institute and
       State University, Ball State University, Empire State
       College, Montana State University, Queens University,
       Western Michigan University
       Business administration (M.B.A.)—Colorado State University,
       University of Notre Dame, University of Tennessee,
       Lehigh University, National University, Stephens
       College, University of Iowa, University of Tennessee
       Business communication—Jones Education Company,
       International business—National Technological University,
       Project management—George Mason University
Chemistry—Lehigh University
Computer science—Colorado State University, George Mason
       University, Oklahoma State University, Stanford
       University, University of California—Santa Barbara,

University of Iowa, University of Massachusetts—
Amherst, University of Nebraska
Computer Information Systems—University of Phoenix
Creative Writing—Goddard College
Families—A*DEC
Finance—American College
Ecological studies—Goddard College
Economics—Empire State College, New Jersey Institute of Technology
Education—Goddard College, Graduate School of America,
Indiana University, Oklahoma State University,
University of New England, Walden University
Adult learning—Graduate School of America, Indiana
University, Pennsylvania State University
Educational leadership and change—Fielding Institute,
Jones Educational Company, University of Maine
Higher education/higher education leadership—University
of Iowa
Human development in technology—George Washington
University
Instructional design—Graduate School of America, Nova
Southeastern University
Distance learning—Graduate School of America, Nova
Southeastern University
Science education—University of Iowa
Speech and language pathology—Nova Southeastern
University
Engineering—Auburn University, National Technological University,
Stanford University, Stevens Institute of Technology,
University of Houston, University of Idaho, Virginia
Polytechnic Institute and State University, Worcester
Polytechnic Institute
Aerospace engineering—Rensselaer Polytechnic Institute,
University of Virginia
Agricultural engineering—Colorado State University
Biological engineering—University of Idaho
Chemical engineering—Colorado State University, Lehigh
University, Oklahoma State University, University of
Virginia
Civil engineering—Colorado State University, University of
Virginia, Virginia Polytechnic Institute and State
University

Computer engineering—University of California—Santa
    Barbara, University of Iowa, University of
    Massachusetts—Amherst
Electrical engineering—Arizona State University, Colorado
    State University, Georgia Institute of Technology,
    Oklahoma State University, Purdue University,
    University of California—Santa Barbara, University of
    Houston, University of Iowa, University of
    Massachusetts—Amherst, University of Virginia,
    Virginia Polytechnic Institute and State University
Engineering management—Colorado State University, New
    Jersey Institute of Technology, Southern
    Methodist University
Fire protection engineering—Worcester Polytechnic Institute
Environmental engineering—Colorado State University,
    Georgia Institute of Technology
Geological engineering—University of Idaho
Hazardous and waste materials management—Southern
    Methodist University
Industrial engineering—Colorado State University, Georgia
    Institute of Technology, Purdue University, University
    of Houston, University of Nebraska, Virginia
    Polytechnic Institute and State University
Information technology and engineering—Florida State
    University, George Mason University
Management of fire protection and engineering—Worcester
    Polytechnic Institute
Manufacturing engineering—Boston University, GMI
    Engineering and Management Institute, Rensselaer
    Polytechnic Institute
Material science engineering—University of Virginia
Mechanical engineering—Colorado State University, Georgia
    Institute of Technology, Oklahoma State University,
    Purdue University, Rensselaer Polytechnic Institute,
    University of Virginia, Virginia Polytechnic Institute
    and State University
Metallurgical engineering—University of Idaho
Mining engineering—University of Idaho
Nuclear and radiological engineering—University of Florida
Quality engineering—Lehigh University
Software systems engineering—George Mason University,
    Southern Methodist University

Structural engineering—University of Virginia
Systems engineering—Colorado State University,
　　　Massachusetts Institute of Technology, Southern
　　　Methodist University, University of Nebraska,
　　　University of Virginia
English—New Jersey Institute of Technology
Environment
　　　Environmental health and safety management—Rochester
　　　　　Institute of Technology
Feminist studies—Goddard College
Health
　　　Health care—International School of Management
　　　Health physics—Georgia Institute of Technology
　　　Health and safety management—Rochester Institute of
　　　　　Technology
　　　Health systems administration—Clarkson University,
　　　　　Rochester Institute of Technology
　　　Health systems finance—Rochester Institute of Technology
　　　Integrated health systems—Rochester Institute of Technology
　　　Public health and health services—George Mason University
　　　Rehabilitation counseling—University of Alabama
History—New Jersey Institute of Technology
Humanities—California State University—Dominguez Hills
Human resources—A*DEC (Colorado State University), Graduate
　　　School of America
Industrial and labor relations—Cornell University
Instruction and performance training—Boise State University
Interdisciplinary studies—Goddard College
International relations—Salve Regina University
Journalism—University of Memphis, University of Nebraska
Labor and policy studies—Empire State College
Liberal arts—Empire State College, University of Maine
Library science—Syracuse University
Literature—Goddard College, New Jersey Institute of Technology
Management—American College, Colorado State University,
　　　Graduate School of America, Massachusetts Institute
　　　of Technology, Rochester Institute of Technology, Salve
　　　Regina University, Thomas Edison State College
　　　Applied management and decision sciences—Walden
　　　　　University
　　　Correctional instititutions—Salve Regina University
　　　Insurance management—Salve Regina University

Information management—International School of
Management, New Jersey Institute of Technology,
Syracuse University
Manufacturing management—GMI Engineering and
Management Institute
Organizational management—University of Phoenix
Global management—University of Phoenix
Technology management—National Technological University,
Rensselaer Polytechnic Institute, University of Phoenix
Telecommunications management—Oklahoma State
University
Marketing—Empire State College, New Jersey Institute of
Technology
Mathematics
Statistics—Colorado State University
Technical mathematics—University of Idaho
Media and communication—Goddard College
Nursing—Indiana University, University of Tennessee, University of
Texas at Tyler
Nutrition—A*DEC
Organizational design—Fielding Institute
Performing arts—Goddard College
Pharmacy—University of Florida, University of Iowa
Philosophy—Union Institute
Psychology
Clinical psychology—Fielding Institute
Human facto psychology—University of Idaho
Psychology and counseling—Goddard College
Physics—University of South Carolina
Professional studies—Cornell University
Public relations—University of Memphis
Quality assurance—California State University—Dominguez Hills
Social ecology—Goddard College
Social policy—Empire State College
Social work—University of Iowa
Software development and management—Rochester Institute of
Technology
Statistics—Colorado State University, George Mason University
Tax law—University of Alabama
Technology
Educational technology leadership—Jones Education
Company (George Washington University)

Instructional technology—New York Institute of Technology
Technology management—National Technological University,
University of Phoenix, University of Waterloo
Telecommunications—Oklahoma State University, Southern
Methodist University, Stevens Institute of Technology
Writing—Goddard College

Index by School Name

Index by Delivery System

Asynchronous communications—Athabasca University, Boise State University, Graduate School of America, Jones Educational Company, Salve Regina University, Stanford University, University of Florida

Audio—interactive—Montana State University, University of California—Santa Barbara

Audiobridge—Nova Southeastern University, University of Virginia, Virginia Polytechnic Institute and State University

Audio cassette—Clarkson College, University of Texas at Tyler

Audioconference—A*DEC

Audiographics—Louisiana State University

Broadcasts—A*DEC, PBS Adult Learning Satellite Service, University of Maine

Bulletin board systems (BBS)—Boise State University

Chat (computerized)—Cornell University, National University, Rochester Institute of Technology, University of Florida, University of Waterloo

CD-ROM—National University

Compressed digital transmission—Cornell University

CompuServe—Embry-Riddle Aeronautical University

Correspondance—Goddard College, Indiana University

E-mail—Empire State College, Massachusetts Institute of Technology, National Technological University, New Jersey Institute of Technology, Rochester Institute of Technology, Salve Regina University, University of New England, Worcester Polytechnic Institute

Fax—Clarkson College, Massachusetts Institute of Technology, New Jersey Institute of Technology

Fiberoptics—New York Institute of Technology, Oklahoma State University

Internet/World Wide Web—A*DEC, Athabasca University, Clarkson College, Empire State College, Fielding Institute, Graduate School of America, Indiana University, International School of Management, Massachusetts Institute of Technology, National Technological University, National University, New Jersey Institute of Technology, New York Institute of Technology, Nova Southeastern University, PBS Adult Learning Satellite Service, Purdue University, Rochester Institute of Technology, Salve Regina University, Stephens College, Stevens Institute of Technology, Syracuse University, Thomas Edison State University, University of Florida, Univerity of Houston, University of Idaho, University of Idaho, University of Maine, University of Nebraska, University of Phoenix, University of Virginia, University of Waterloo, Walden University, Worcester Polytechnic Institute

Microwave—Sanford University, University of Idaho

On-site instruction—Fielding Institute, University of Tennessee

Printed materials—Clarkson College, Empire State College, University of Idaho, University of Waterloo

Residency—Empire State College, Goddard College, Stephens College, Thomas Edison State University, Union Institute

Satellite—A*DEC, Ball State University, California State University—Dominguez Hills, Cornell University, Lehigh University, Louisiana State University, National Technological University, Oklahoma State University, PBS Adult Learning Satellite Service, Purdue University, Rensselaer Polytechnic Institute, University of Houston, University of Idaho, University of Nebraska, University of Virginia, Virginia Polytechnic Institute and State University

Telecommunications network—Purdue University, Walden University

Teleconferencing—National University

Telephone—New Jersey Institute of Technology, University of Maine, University of Waterloo

Teleresponder—Ball State University

Television
  Cable television—Arizona State University, California State
      University—Dominguez Hills, George Washington
      University, Jones Education Company, University of
      Maine
  Digital television—Ball State University, California State
      University—Dominguez Hills, Cornell University,
      Lehigh University
  Interactive television—Florida State University, Indiana
      University, University of Maine
Video—Colorado State University, Cornell University, National
      University, New Jersey Institute of Technology,
      University of Houston
  Compressed video—Louisiana State University, New York
      Institute of Technology, Stanford University, University
      of Houston, University of Idaho, University of Notre
      Dame, University of Texas at Tyler, Univerity of
      Virginia, Western Michigan University
  Interactive Video—Montana State University, New Jersey
      Institute of Technology, Pennsylvania State University,
      Stevens Institute of Technology, University of
      California—Santa Barbara, University of Tennessee
  Videoconference—A*DEC, Boston University, Massachusetts
      Institute of Technology, Queens University,
      Rensselaer Polytechnic Institute, University of
      Alabama, University of Illinois, Worcester Polytechnic
      Institute
  Videotape—Auburn University, Clarkson College, Embry-
      Riddle Aeronautical University, Georgia Institute of
      Technology, GMI Engineering and Management
      Institute, Purdue University, Rensselaer Polytechnic
      Institute, Rochester Institute of Technology, Southern
      Methodist University, Stanford University, University
      of Alabama, University of California—Santa Barbara
      University of Florida, University of Idaho, University of
      Maine, University of Massachusetts—Amherst,
      University of New England, University of South
      Carolina, University of Texas at Tyler, Western
      Michigan University, Worcester Polytechnic Institute
Voice Mail—Clarkson College

Notes

Notes

Notes

Want more information about our services, products, or the nearest Kaplan educational center?

HERE

Call our nationwide toll-free numbers:

1-800-KAP-TEST
(for information on our live courses, private tutoring and admissions consulting)

1-800-KAP-ITEM
(for information on our products)

1-888-KAP-LOAN*
(for information on student loans)

Connect with us in cyberspace:
On **AOL**, keyword **"Kaplan"**
On the Internet's World Wide Web, open **"http://www.kaplan.com"**
Via E-mail, **"info@kaplan.com"**

Write to:
Kaplan Educational Centers
888 Seventh Avenue
New York, NY 10106